GW00401308

HOUSEHOLD
HINTS

Emma Andrews

SUMMERSDALE

Copyright © Summersdale Publishers 1995

All rights reserved.

No part of this book may be reproduced by any means, nor transmitted, nor translated into a machine language, without the written permission of the publisher.

Summersdale Publishers
46 West Street
Chichester
PO19 1RP
England

A CIP catalogue record for this book is available from the British Library.

Printed and bound in Great Britain
by Selwood Printing Ltd.

ISBN 1 873475 14 4

Original illustrations by Sophie Sitwell.

Important note:
All reasonable care has been taken to ensure that the hints in this book are safe and workable. The author and the publishers cannot accept any responsibility for any proceedings or prosecutions brought or instituted against any person or body as a result of the use or misuse of any of the hints outlined in this book or any loss, injury or damage caused thereby.

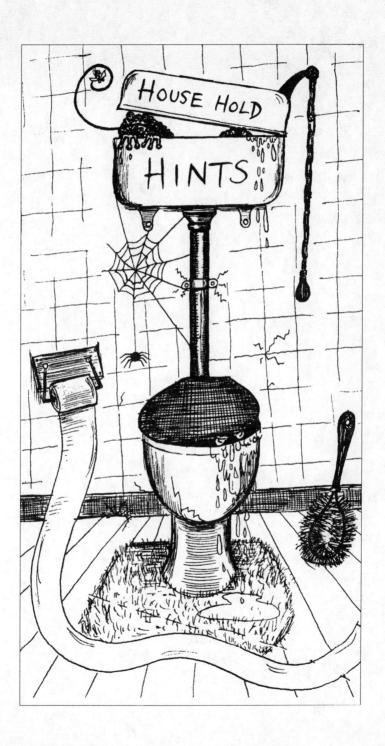

Contents

Introduction

If you have a household to run, you know what an endless uphill struggle it can be to keep things under control. If you seem to spend your whole life cleaning the house or attempting to keep your house in order, this is the book you have been waiting for. It is designed to make your life easier, showing how to use your time more efficiently, giving you more time to pursue your hobbies or to relax.

Hints like these are lessons that have been learnt through the experience of many people over many years. Household hints are normally passed from generation to generation, and from friend to friend. Bit by bit we accumulate knowledge on how to live in a modern society with all its gadgets, responsibilities and complications. This book represents a valuable short-cut to that knowledge, an easily accessible volume of vital information from which anyone could benefit.

The Organised House

There have been many changes in the way that households are organised and run; these changes are mainly due to technological advances and social changes. The last century has seen a prolific increase in the design and availability of many household appliances. Most houses in this country have at least a Hoover and a washing machine and it would be hard to imagine life without them, but only 50 years ago both would have been a luxury that few could afford. There is no doubt that running a household was a full-time occupation in those days, (anyone who does not have a washing machine will know how time consuming it is washing clothes by hand). Apart from technological advances there have been a number of important social changes that have had a significant effect on the household. Families are, on average, smaller in size than they were, this means that there is theoretically less work to do.

Women have always traditionally been regarded as the homemakers, with the man of the house being the 'bread winner'. Tradition has now been flung aside, to give way to a change in the stereotypical roles that were once dominant. Household chores are usually shared by both partners, although there is an ever increasing number of men who stay at home while their partner goes out to work and they take full charge of the domestic responsibilities. With this in mind the book is aimed at both sexes and all ages.

Whatever the size of your house and family and regardless of whether you have all the latest household gadgets, there are still a number of tasks that have to be done in order to keep the home looking clean and tidy. Unfortunately there is never enough time to do all that we want, so sacrifices have to be made. Do you do the ironing or do you go out with friends? We all know what we would prefer to do but sometimes it gets to the stage where there are certain onerous tasks that must be attended to.

Running a home is an occupation in itself: if you have teenage children and you leave them on their own for a few days, by the time you return your house will be even more unrecognisable than it normally is. But if you, your house and your household is organised, things need not be so bad. A little efficiency and organisation will save you time, money and emotional strain: all you have to do is follow some of the golden rules in this book. One of the most important of these rules is to keep calm: it is very hard to be organised if you get in a flap every time something goes wrong.

How to be organised
Guarantees
This information also refers to receipts and instructions for appliances: there are many occasions when you need to produce documentary evidence of the purchase of a product. It might be because you want to return it to the shop or the manufacturer, or

for insurance purchases. Keep them in a safe place where you will be able to find them when needed.

Lists

It is worth buying scribble boards that you can wipe clean. They are useful for writing down things that you have to do, such as cleaning jobs, items of shopping or a dentist's appointment. Whatever it might be, if it is written down you are less likely to forget it.

Messages

If you live in a busy household there are going to be times when messages don't get passed on. How many times have you taken a phone message intending to write it down or pass it on and then it completely slips your mind? Have a pad of paper by the phone with a pen tied SECURELY to it: use the thickest chains possible, as pens are notorious as the Houdinis of the stationery world.

Children

Children can give you a lifetime of pleasure. Allegedly. On the other hand children can create chaos within minutes. They are demanding, difficult and noisy (those are their good points). Depending on the age of your children you will encounter different problems, and I am not even going to contemplate giving any advice as there is simply not enough room in a book of this nature. What I will do is suggest a few tips that can help make things run a little more smoothly if you have children.

Young children

• Try to instil a few ground rules even at an early age. Teach them not to leave their toys lying around: it can be a real hazard, especially in the kitchen.

• Keep sheets of paper and coloured pens at hand to keep your children amused.

• When the children are older make a list of telephone numbers of their friends in case you need to contact your child in an emergency.

• Keep a list of any allergies your children have, especially allergies to medication. Also keep an up to date list of inoculations. This will save you time trying to remember which of your children has had measles etc. It is not always easy to remember these things, especially if you have a large family.

• Keep a list of medical appointments on a notice board, so you don't forget when to take your children.

• Try to encourage your children to undertake extra curricula activities such as music lessons and sports. Although children should never be forced into activities they do not want to do (except washing up), there are times when they contemplate giving up a pastime because they feel it is too difficult. This is when strong encouragement should be given as they will probably end up thanking you later on.

Safety tips

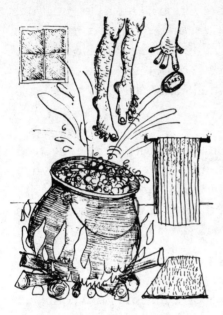

Each year there is an alarming number of horrific accidents that occur in the home: fires, scaldings, broken bones, electrocutions, etc. This might sound a little dramatic but it is the unfortunate reality.

It is also true that many accidents that occur in the home are avoidable if care is taken. You must be aware of the potential hazards that could happen, if you have children you should be even more conscious as children and accidents seem to go hand in hand.

In connection with safety in the home, make sure that you read the section on first aid and have at least a basic first aid kit. Most accidents that occur are not life threatening, but are more likely to be things like breaking a plate or glass and cutting a finger. Each area of the house has its own particular hazards as well as more general ones.

The Kitchen

This is the scene of numerous accidents. Many are minor, others are more serious. Due to its function, ie. food preparation, there are a number of dangerous ingredients around: I'm not talking about food, more like knives, food processors, boiling water etc. Safety in the kitchen is essential, so here are a few guidelines.

Knives

• Sharp knives are not necessarily more dangerous than blunt ones. A blunt knife can slip off when cutting food, especially things like tomatoes; they also require more force and will tear certain food such as meat. A sharp knife will give a nice clean cut.

• Never use a big knife for a small job and vice versa. A very cheap kitchen knife can bend when cutting tough objects, so it is worth investing in a couple of well made kitchen knives. Many accidents in the kitchen involve cuts from knives: this is usually due to a lack of care. A tip is to cut the way chefs do, that is move your fingers back with the knife so they are never in the line of the knife blade. If you have a friend in the catering business ask them to show you, as it is not that hard to learn.

• Take care if you store your kitchen knives in a drawer or when you are washing them up: if you are groping blindly you can cut yourself when trying to pick them up, so invest in a knife block.

Pans

• If you have ever had the misfortune to be holding a saucepan of boiling hot water and then seconds later you are only left holding the handle and the contents of the saucepan are on the floor or even over you, you will know how hazardous a loose handle can be. Make sure that you regularly tighten the handles on all your pans.

• Take care with the positioning of pans on your cooker. Remember to keep the handles from protruding over the edge of the cooker otherwise they could be knocked over. The safest way is to use the rear hobs rather than the front ones. If you have children make sure that they do not run around in the kitchen when cooking is going on.

Kitchen gadgets

There is an increasing choice of kitchen gadgets: blenders, mixers, juicers, and processors. Many of them can be dangerous if used incorrectly. The golden rule is never try to cut corners - you might end up cutting your fingers off because many of these implements have very sharp motorised blades. When you are using a food processor make sure that you never feed in food while the blade is rotating. Always turn off a machine at the power point before changing blades.

Storage

A well organised kitchen is normally a safe kitchen. Keep heavy items in low cupboards and lighter items in high cupboards. If you keep all your heavy pans in a high cupboard you will be risking injury every time you reach up to retrieve them. Never use a stool to stand on if you are trying to reach an object, even a chair can be unstable. Ideally you should have a small kitchen step ladder.

Fire in the kitchen

The most common type of fire in a kitchen is a fat fire. It can easily happen: you have a pan of fat on the cooker, the phone rings and you go off to answer it, forgetting all about the fat, and a few moments later your kitchen could be ablaze. When oil begins to smoke you know it is very hot and could ignite at any moment. If you do have a fat fire there are certain important ways of dealing with it.

Rule one
● Never pour on water directly to the oil. This is very hazardous and makes the fire worse.

Rule two
● Turn off the heat.

Rule three
● Place a damp cloth over the top of the pan and leave until you are certain that the fire is extinguished.

If you have a fire in the oven turn off the heat but don't open the door of the oven. If you keep the door closed the fire will extinguish itself when the supply of oxygen is used up.

Other hazards
Electrical
There are two main hazards: fires and shocks, both potentially serious.

Electrical fires can be caused by the main wiring in the house, overloaded power points, or faulty wiring on individual appliances.

● If you have an old house and you feel that there is a problem with the wiring, ie. the lights start flickering or switches get warm, get help. Call an electrician to come and take a look: it could be serious.

● Never have too many appliances on a multi plug. It could overload it and cause an electrical fire.

● Make sure that all your appliances have the right fuse fitted. The fuse acts as a power breaker if there is a short circuit or electrical surge. If the wrong fuse is fitted you risk ruining the appliance and your life. Some people when they run out of fuses use a piece of foil to make the circuit: this is extremely foolish, dangerous and should never be done.

● Certain appliances need different fuses depending on how much current they draw.

Up to 600 watts use a 3 amp. fuse.
600 to 1000 watts use a 5 amp. fuse.
Over a 1000 watts use a 13 amp. fuse.

The appliance should give instructions as to what fuse must be fitted.

● Choosing the correct fuse is not the only part of electrical safety. Make sure that in lamps you do not use a light bulb with too high a wattage for the lampshade. If you use a high wattage bulb it could cause the lampshade to catch fire if it is only designed to take a low wattage bulb.

• Make sure if you are wiring an appliance yourself that you use the correct wire. Some thin wires may melt if they are used with an appliance that requires a lot of power.

• Before attempting to repair anything electrical make sure that the power is turned off.

• Never strip the wire back so that wires are exposed outside of the plug and don't forget to use the cable grips that are on a plug. Their purpose is to stop the wires from being pulled out if the flex is being stretched.

• Take care with electrical products that you have purchased abroad. They will normally run on a different voltage, so check with an electrician if in any doubt.

• Try to remember to switch appliances off at the power points when they are not in use. This will not only lessen the chance of an electrical fire it will also save you money as most appliances still draw power even when they are on stand-by.

• If there is a part of the flex that has frayed or split, then have it repaired or preferably replaced.

• When touching electrical appliances make sure that your hands and the appliance are dry.

Electric Blankets

These should be used with care. Make sure that the blanket lies flat and is tied to the bed. If it is creased, it could cause the element to break.

- Do not use a hot water bottle and an electric blanket together.

- Do not dry clean electric blankets.

- Make sure the correct fuse is fitted.

Power Cuts

During a power cut go round turning off appliances such as electric fires, electric hobs, irons etc, because you might forget they are on when the power returns and they could cause a fire.

Gas appliances

There is just as much potential for accidents involving gas appliances as there is for electrical ones, so care must be taken.

- If you buy a second-hand gas appliance it must be checked by a qualified engineer, and even a gas cooker must be fitted by a engineer.

- Do not use instant water heaters for a period of more than five minutes at a time, as they are not designed for this purpose.

- If you have gas heaters make sure that there is adequate ventilation for the fumes that are omitted.

- Do not block air vents in rooms to stop draughts. They are needed to provide ventilation.

• If you have a gas water heater in the bathroom do not get into the bath while the water is still running.

• Have your gas appliances regularly serviced by a qualified engineer. It is recommended that an engineer is used who is a member of the Confederation for the Registration of Gas Installers (CORGI) or is authorised by British Gas.

What to do if you smell gas

The first thing to do is to decide whether the smell of gas is strong or faint. Although it is always advisable never to take any risks when gas is involved, there are simple causes of gas leaks that are not serious if they are dealt with quickly and in a safe manner.

Faint smell of gas

• If you smell gas in the home check that you have not left any gas rings on unlit and the same with the oven.

• Check pilot lights to gas appliances such as cookers and boilers.

• Extinguish any naked flames, including cigarettes.

• Ventilate the room by opening windows and doors.

• Relight any pilot lights that had gone out once the smell of gas has definitely gone. Keep an eye on the pilot as it might go out again.

• If the smell of gas persists and you are unable to find an explanation then turn the gas off at the mains and call the gas board.

Strong smell of gas

- Open all exterior doors and windows.

- Turn the gas off at the mains.

- Extinguish any naked flames and switch off any electric fires.

- Contact the gas board regardless of the time.

- Do not turn on or off any electrical switches other than those for an electric fire.

- Do not stay in a room which smells very strongly of gas.

More safety tips

There are literally hundreds of potential perils in the home, but this does not mean that you have to be paranoid about it. All you need to be is aware and make sure that your home is a safe place to live in.

- Make sure that your home is adequately lit especially in areas such as the stairs and landing.

- Make sure that you never use old drink bottles to store hazardous chemicals, as it is possible they might be mistaken for the original item. This is very important if you have young children.

- Keep all medicine, chemicals and matches out of the reach of children.

- Never polish the area of floor where a rug is placed, if you do the rug could slip and cause an accident.

- If you spill something in the kitchen, especially if it is oily, clear it up straight away as it could cause someone to slip over.

• If you have a broken glass or china to dispose of make sure that it is wrapped carefully otherwise it could cause the dustmen serious injury.

• Some chemicals produce harmful gases, so make sure that when using chemicals you read the instructions and have adequate ventilation.

The bathroom

The bathroom also has many potential hazards: elderly people, for instance, tend to be susceptible to accidents getting in and out of the bath. A rubber mat in the bottom of the bath should help to stop any slipping. Hand rails can also be fitted in strategic places to aid getting in and out of the bath. These can also be fitted by the side of the toilet.

Other tips

• Never leave a young child alone in the bath.

• Don't take any electrical appliances in the bathroom, such as televisions or radios.

• Make sure that you have pull cords for lights and heaters, not ordinary switches as they are dangerous and illegal.

• In case an accident occurs it is best if you don't lock the door of the bathroom. If there are children living in the house, place the bathroom door lock high on the door, out of their reach, so that they can't lock themselves in.

Fire in the house

This can be a frightening experience however small the fire. It is important to be aware of both how to deal with this kind of emergency and how best to prevent it from happening in the first place.

Precautions:

● Smoke alarms should be fitted throughout the house and tested on a regular basis.

● A fire blanket should be kept in the kitchen.

● Make sure that the keys to door and window locks are kept in an accessible place in case they are needed in a hurry.

● If using a 'real' fire in any room, place a fireguard in front of it whenever leaving the room. Sparks and embers frequently jump out of the grate and onto the carpet, even after the fire has gone out, and these are major causes of house fires. Also make sure the chimney is swept regularly: chimney fires can occur when too much soot has built up.

● See section on electrical and gas safety for further advice on avoiding fires.

In the event of a chimney fire:

● Extinguish the fire in the grate and call the fire brigade.

● To stop any soot falling onto the floor, put a fireguard in place.

• Remove any furniture that is near the fireplace, and if the room is getting smoky remove any other items that might be susceptible to smoke damage.

In event of a house fire:
• Attempt to put out the fire if there is no risk of getting hurt. If you feel that the fire is beyond control phone the fire brigade.

• You can use water on most fires except electrical and oil. However water can be used to extinguish an oil heater fire. Stand well clear of the appliance when using water to extinguish the fire.

• See the section on kitchen safety for advice on kitchen fires.

• If you think that there is a fire present behind a door, ie. there are signs of smoke seeping from the edges, the utmost care must be taken. Feel the door: if the door is hot the fire could be close to the door and it could be dangerous to open it. If you have to open the door because it is the only exit, open it a small amount keeping a firm hold on the door to stop it from being forced open.

• If there is a fire in the house that is producing fumes and smoke, get as low as you can on the floor and make your way to an exit. Fires thrive on air so close all doors and windows if you have a chance, but never put yourself at risk.

• If you are stuck in a room with no safe way out, first of all try to block any gaps in the door using pieces of clothing. If you can wet them first it is more effective. Do not leap out of an upstairs window until you have to, there is no point in risking breaking your back if you might be rescued before the fire reaches you.

• If your clothing is set alight, try to smother the flames either by rolling on the floor or smothering with a blanket. Fire burns upwards, remember, so always get on the floor if your clothes are burning. This will keep the flames away from your face and hair.

• Although it will be difficult, try to keep calm.

Safety tips in the garden and garage

It is not only the house that is a site of potential hazards, care must be taken in the garden and the garage.

• When gardening always wear suitable footwear: if you are only wearing flimsy shoes they will provide little protection against the sharp blades of a lawnmower or even a garden fork.

• Put away all tools after use. If you leave tools lying around when it gets dark not only will they become rusty but you or a member of your family might trip over them. One of the worst culprits is the garden hose, so always coil it away after use. Treading on a rake and being hit on the nose by its handle may be funny, but it hurts.

• When using power tools always use a circuit breaker. This cuts the power off immediately if there is a problem with the wiring, ie. if the lead is cut or shorts out.

• Keep insecticides and poisons out of reach of children and pets.

First Aid

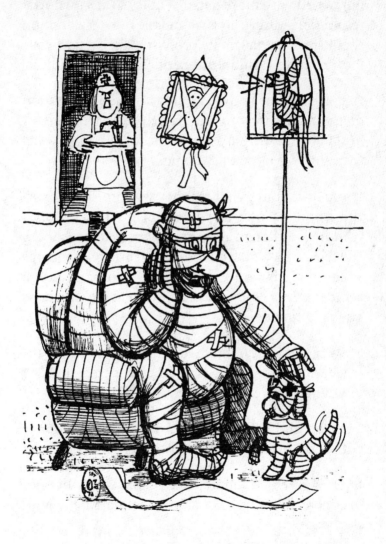

A basic knowledge of first aid is important. Not only is it in your own interest, you might also be in the position to help other people. The following chapter only gives a limited amount of information and it is recommended that a specialist first aid book is purchased with more detail. Topics such as artificial respiration, cardiac massage and the recovery position should really be taught by professionals. Contact your local St. John's Ambulance service for further advice.

Accidents in the home account for a high proportion of the admissions to the casualty departments of hospitals. But there are many types of minor accidents that can be dealt with at home.

If you have young children they will probably regard the home as one large adventure playground. Children, although remarkably resilient to knocks and falls, are at risk from other potentially dangerous situations. Many accidents in the home could be avoided if more care is taken and the home is made as safe as it can be.

How safe is your home? Do you have smoke alarms fitted? Are your medicines and poisons out of reach of young children? Is the wiring safe?

See the section on safety in the home for more details on making your home safe.

Every household should have at least a basic first aid kit. Here are a few essentials that should be kept in the house:

First Aid Kit:
1) Box of assorted plasters, for grazes and minor cuts.
2) Packet of sterilised cotton wool.
3) 1 roll of surgical tape.

4) At least 2 tubular gauze bandages.
5) 2 Large triangular bandages.
6) Two packs of wound dressings, sizes medium and large.
7) Scissors.
6) Safety pins.
8) Tweezers.
9) Pin.
10) Antiseptic cream.

Other items that should be kept in a medicine chest :

1) Thermometer.
2) Antihistamine cream.
3) Indigestion tablets.
4) Aspirin or paracetamol.
5) Calamine lotion.
6) Medicine spoon.

Here are a few possible situations which could arise in and around the home that require first aid treatment. If you are ever in doubt as to whether you or a member of your family requires hospital treatment, don't take any chances: take them straight to the hospital or call an ambulance if you lack transport or if it might be dangerous to move the patient.

Bites and Stings
We are all susceptible to bites and stings from insects and animals. Some are harmless, but others require careful treatment.

Bites

Thankfully in Britain we are still free from the rabies virus, but bites from animals can still require medical attention. If the wound is only superficial it can be dealt with at home.

• Clean the wound with soap and water and apply a dressing. If the wound becomes infected or does not heal consult your doctor.

• If the bite has punctured the skin, just wash the wound and visit the casualty department of your local hospital.

• Insect stings such as bee or wasp stings are common. It is possible for people to have an allergic reaction to stings and they can prove to be fatal in rare cases. Anyone who is allergic to stings should seek medical attention immediately if stung.

• Stings in general should be treated with an antihistamine cream, or ice packs. Some people find vinegar effective!

• *One tip: squeezing a sting will not help, it will only spread the sting. If you are stung by a bee it is possible to remove the sting if you have a pair of tweezers.*

Bleeding

Please note that tourniquets should not be applied around a limb, unless you are trained in their use. A badly applied tourniquet can cause more harm than good. Usually minor cuts and grazes will stop bleeding of their own accord when the clotting process takes effect.

To stop bleeding:
Cuts and grazes
● Sit or lie your patient down, and wash your hands if possible before beginning treatment.

● Allow to bleed for a few seconds to allow any foreign bodies to wash away from the entrance to the wound. Then apply pressure to wound with a clean dressing until bleeding stops.

● When the wound has stopped bleeding, apply a clean dressing. If you know that there is a foreign body in the wound don't put a dressing directly over the top of the wound, use a ring bandage, so there is no direct pressure on the wound.

● If the bleeding is severe try to raise the injured part so that gravity will draw some of the blood supply away.

● Press hard on the wound with a clean handkerchief or something similar. Do this for about ten minutes.

● Apply another clean dressing. If the blood seeps through put another dressing on top. Never take the old dressing off. Seek medical assistance.

Bruises
When bleeding occurs beneath the skin, usually as a result of a knock or a fall, the skin appears a blue colour and there is normally associated swelling.

● The pain and swelling can be treated with a cold compress or ice bag.

Burns and Scalds

Children are susceptible to burns and scalding: it is important that the procedure for treating burns is familiar to you. A burn that covers 10% or more of the body can cause shock due to the loss of plasma.

● If you are on the scene when the scald occurs try to remove any article of clothing that is in contact with the burn, as any clothing will keep the heat in. Forget this if the clothes have already cooled.

● Don't remove burnt clothing as it will have been sterilised by the fire.

● Remove any item of clothing that has been in contact with corrosive chemicals, but make sure you protect yourself from getting burnt.

● Hold the burnt area under cool running water. If the area is too large keep it cool by drenching it with water.

● Remove any constricting items from a burnt area, eg. shoes, belts or rings before the swelling appears.

● Shock is a common secondary phenomenon after being burnt and must be treated.

Choking

Children are again prone to choking: the cause can be any foreign object such as a piece of food or even a small toy. But it is not just children who can choke, it can happen to anyone.

• When someone is choking try to manoeuvre the person so that their head is lower than their chest (if possible).

• If the person is coughing it means that the airway is not completely blocked. If they are turning blue then it is likely that the airway is almost entirely blocked.

• The first line of treatment is to hit the patient between the shoulder blades with the heel of the hand. If this is not successful try to remove the obstructing object with a finger.

• If you cannot remove the item then it is imperative to get the person to hospital as quickly as possible.

Electric Shock
Domestic electric shocks are normally caused by faulty appliances, and can be deadly. The strength of the shock depends not only on the voltage and the current, but also the conductor. For example if you have wet hands you will receive a more severe shock than if you have dry hands, as water is a good conductor of electricity. An electric shock can cause severe burns as well as stopping the heart.

• Never touch a person who has received an electric shock until the source of the electricity has been turned off, otherwise you will receive a shock too.

• If it is not possible to switch off the current, try to move the person away from contact with the electrical item. Before you do this, position yourself on a non-conducting surface, for example, layers of dry newspaper or cardboard and then using a non-conducting object such as a wooden broom handle try to break the contact.

• If the casualty appears unconscious, check for signs of breathing and a pulse. If the casualty is breathing but unconscious, place in the recovery position.

• If the patient is not breathing commence with artificial respiration.

• If you cannot feel a pulse, proceed with external cardiac massage, but only if you have had training in this technique, do not attempt this if you have no experience in this area.

Faints
Fainting is a common phenomenon, usually caused by a reduced supply of blood to the brain. If you feel faint, loosen any tight clothing, lie, or sit down with your head between your knees. Use the same procedure if you see someone feeling faint.

• If they have trouble breathing and remain feeling faint place the patient in the recovery position.

Foreign Bodies
Young children are prone to placing small objects in their ears or up their noses

Ears
• If you can see the object try to remove it with your fingers or a pair of tweezers, but never poke about in the ear canal.

Eyes

● Only try to remove a foreign body if it is in the white part of the eye, if elsewhere take the patient to casualty. To remove an object from the white part of the eye, either flush out using an eye bath, or use a wet cotton wool bud and gently remove it.

Nose

● If an object is stuck in the nose, instruct the child to breathe through its mouth and take it to casualty where they will have the appropriate instruments to remove the object.

Poisoning

This can be serious and quick action is required to avoid great harm from being done.

It is mainly children who are susceptible to poisoning and every effort must be made to stop them from gaining access to poisons and medicines in the first place.

● Try to find out what poison has been taken so that the hospital can give the most appropriate form of treatment.

● Poisons can be classified into either corrosive or non-corrosive. Domestic chemicals such as bleach and other cleaning products are corrosive, whereas medicines can be non-corrosive.

Treatment for corrosives

If the poison that was taken was a corrosive there will be signs of burns around the mouth and pain will be felt in the stomach.

• Contrary to popular belief the victim should not be made to vomit as this can cause more damage.

• Give the victim water or milk if the poison is an acid: this helps to dilute the poison. If the poison is an alkali, lemon juice should be given.

• Clean the area around the mouth with a wet cloth.

• Call an ambulance.

Treatment for non-corrosives
• Make sure that the victim is still conscious, check breathing and pulse. If they are unconscious place in the recovery position. If conscious try to induce vomiting.

• Take a sample of the vomit to give to the ambulanceman.

• Call an ambulance.

In the kitchen

Good kitchen practice

A kitchen must be kept scrupulously clean and well organised. There are a number of health risks that occur if a kitchen is dirty or food is left to go off. Food poisoning is caused by harmful bacteria such as salmonella, but there are many other types that can cause illness.

Kitchen tips

• Never leave out food that should be kept in the fridge. After shopping, especially in the summer, make sure that food is put in the fridge or freezer as soon after purchase as possible. Bacteria quickly grow in warm conditions, whereas in the fridge their growth is impeded.

• Never buy any perishable product that you feel might not be fresh.

• Wash all fruit, vegetables and salad produce.

• When cooking make sure that the food is completely cooked. There are exceptions as some meat and fish is eaten raw or partially cooked. When eating food of this nature it is vital that the produce is as fresh as possible - don't take any chances.

• When reheating food make sure that it gets hot all the way through before serving.

Freezing

The freezer is one of the most useful of household appliances. It works by preventing the food from decay caused by bacteria. The speed at which the food is frozen is important. Small ice crystals are formed when food is frozen quickly, but the slower it is frozen the bigger the ice crystals become. Many freezers have a fast freeze section which is there for a purpose: if the food is frozen slowly large ice crystals form, and when they defrost there is a resultant damage to the cell walls of the food.

• To aid fast freezing do not place large quantities of unfrozen food in the freezer in one go as this will raise the temperature of the freezer and slow the freezing process. Food that has been cooked should be cold before placing in the freezer.

• If you are low on food or you have unexpected guests then there should hopefully be something in the freezer you can use. This is where the problem begins: do you know what is in your freezer and perhaps more importantly how long it has been there?

• It amazes me how some people's freezer contents lack any type of labelling. It is a case of lucky dip or trying to feel what is wrapped up, which is no easy task when the items are frozen.

• So it is essential that your freezer is organised: this will save you time and money.

• Label and date all the items in your freezer. It is also a good idea to keep a separate list on the outside of the freezer door which you can update every time you add or take something out. If you are not doing this already you will find it extremely useful. There will be no excuse for having mysterious packages lying in the bottom of your freezer of which you have no idea what or how old they are. (It can be dangerous to eat food that has been in the freezer for too long.)

● Freezers run more efficiently when they are full so try to keep your freezer well stocked even if it is half full of bread.

● Unless food is adequately wrapped it is susceptible to 'freezer burn', caused by the freezing air that circulates in the freezer.

● When using containers with a lid, remember to leave a space for expansion, otherwise the container may crack.

Thawing food
Whereas food should be frozen as quickly as possible, when it comes to thawing it should be done as slowly as possible. When food is thawed quickly it dries out and some flavour can be lost.

● For health reasons, extra care should be taken when defrosting meat and fish: check that it has defrosted completely before cooking.

Wine

The consumption of wine in this country has steadily increased over the last decade, and with relaxed border controls allowing copious personal imports of the drink most households now keep at least a modest wine rack in their kitchen or cellar.

Choosing wine

As Great Britain produces little wine of its own it relies heavily on imports from many countries. We are fortunate that we have the opportunity to purchase such a wide range of wines. If you are in France it is difficult to buy anything but French produced wine, trying to find a bottle of New Zealand Chardonnay would be almost impossible.

The interest in wine in this country has meant that the days when a bottle of Leibfraumilch served at dinner was thought to be the height of sophistication are long over. Choosing wine is determined by a number of factors, such as taste, budget, what it is being accompanied by etc. Red and white wines are most commonly drunk in this country, with Rosé being another alternative. Although traditionally red wine was always drunk with meat and white with fish, this rule is now frequently flouted as it is all about personal preference. You may not be aware that certain wines such as Beaujolais and Loire reds can be served lightly chilled.

The best way to find out about wine is to experiment, you will soon discover what type of wine you like. You will find that there are many perfectly drinkable bottles of wine that will not break the bank, especially those from Eastern Europe which is beginning to make consistently good wines for relatively little money. Once you get more advanced you will learn about the different grape varieties and how they affect the taste of the wine, and the classification system that exists for French and Italian wines.

Buying wine does not have to be expensive. Years ago wine buying was dominated by stuffy wine merchants; thankfully now there are several high street chains that offer customers value for money, with helpful and knowledgeable staff and often free tastings.

If you wish to learn more about wine invest in one of the many excellent books that are available on this intoxicating subject. Wine tasting as a hobby has got to be one of the most enjoyable pastimes imaginable.

Serving wine
The essence of serving wine is making sure that it is served at the correct temperature, which is almost as important as choosing the wine itself.

White wine
• White wine and Rosé will take about an hour to chill in the fridge or about 20 minutes in an ice bucket. If you have an ice bucket remember to fill it with half ice and half water as it will chill the wine more quickly and you will need fewer ice cubes.

• Never over-chill wine, especially expensive bottles.

Red wine
• Red wine should be served at 'room' temperature, which means about 65°F. If the wine is cool never try to speed up the process by placing it near a fire or in a bowl of boiling water.

• It is normally only wines that are over ten years old that have enough sediment to make decanting worthwhile.

• Open red wine at least an hour before serving to allow the wine to breath.

Entertaining

Some people are naturals at entertaining, whether it be a simple supper for two or a formal dinner for twelve. If you find it something of a challenge, however, there are some simple rules that should be adhered to if you to want make entertaining simple and fun. After all, if you are doing all the hard work, why not enjoy it? The host is ultimately responsible for the happiness of the guests. The host has to fulfil a number of roles: besides preparing and cooking the food, the host will have to look after the guests, make introductions, keep the conversation going if it dries up, and even try to smooth over any disputes that might arise (when planning the seating arrangements think about who is going to get on with who, and keep any 'troublemakers' apart).

It is good to get into the habit of being so organised when entertaining that you can take the time to relax an hour before the guests arrive. I find that taking a shower or bath provides the perfect start to an enjoyable evening, followed by a cool drink and a quick rest. It will make you feel refreshed and charged up for the night. There is nothing worse when you are entertaining than if you are in the kitchen slaving over a hot stove minutes before your guests arrive: you will feel flustered and will certainly look flustered.

Being organised is not as difficult as it might appear and once you get into good habits you will find entertaining a pleasure, much to the envy of any unorganised guests, who will be amazed at the leisurely attitude you take.

Entertaining can be for a number of reasons: it can be for pleasure, business or for a celebration. Whatever the occasion, planning is the secret.

Planning tips:
The Menu
Plan the menu well in advance and keep it simple, don't try to be too adventurous. Being over-ambitious is a recipe for disaster. It is sensible to try a new recipe out before the event, then you will have an idea if it will be suitable. If you don't try it out before hand, it could go horribly wrong, and this would be embarrassing if it was an important occasion. It is often prudent to play it safe and stick to recipes that you know well.

If you do a lot of entertaining keep a diary in which you can record the following:

- The date the occasion took place
- List of guests (any dislikes they might have)
- Food served
- Wine served
- Notes on how the occasion went, ways that the recipes could be improved or whether they should be repeated.

By keeping notes it will save you time when trying to work out if you have ever cooked a certain dish for your guests on a previous occasion. Make sure when you are planning a menu that the ingredients are available, ie. they may be out of season. When planning a menu consider how much preparation a particular dish will take: does it require your constant attention whilst your guests are sitting down? Will it keep if your guests are late?

There is no point having friends to dinner if you are going to spend half the time in the kitchen. It results in a stressed host and an uncomfortable feeling amongst the guests. Here are a few more suggestions that might help.

- Choose dishes that need little supervision and will not spoil if they are served later than planned.

- Never try to produce a menu that is beyond your capabilities.

• The food should look fresh. The fresher it is when bought the fresher it will taste when served. When buying fresh produce, work out how out long it is before you are going to use it and whether it will keep. If you require the use of certain fruit for a recipe you must judge carefully the ripeness at the time of purchase. If you buy fruit that is already ripe but you are not going to use it for several days, it will be past its best when you do use it.

• Keep it simple: if you have trouble with your timing, choose dishes that have only one accompaniment, for example a casserole with rice, and have a starter that you can prepare in advance.

• It is always better to cook too much than too little. Any extra that is left over can always be eaten another day.

Remember that entertaining should be enjoyable, if it is not you must be doing something wrong. Think carefully about your previous efforts and how you could make improvements.

It is not only the food that is important when entertaining, there are certain other factors that contribute to a memorable occasion:

Creating a favourable impression
Entertaining is more than just serving marvellous food: the atmosphere in which it is served is equally important. Obviously it is important to decide on the type of

atmosphere you require, which will depend on the function. If the reason behind the dinner is business then you should try to create a different atmosphere from that for a group of friends.

• Make sure that you have a wide range of drinks to offer your guests, and don't forget to buy mixers.

• If you are serving pre-dinner drinks have a selection of nibbles to offer your guests, but don't go over the top so they lose their appetite for the meal.

• Chill white wines and open red wines in advance of the meal.

• Make sure that you have enough ice cubes and lemon for drinks. If you are having a large number of guests, make trays of ice cubes in advance and then empty the cubes into a plastic bag and keep them in the freezer, this way you will have plenty.

• Make sure that you have enough food and drink (don't forget to have a range of soft drinks for the abstainers and low alcohol drinks for the drivers).

• If you have a real fire make use of it, 'weather permitting'. There is nothing better for creating a warm welcome.

• Try to make the time to do a small table display of flowers. The arrangement should be discrete, not too tall as it could hinder the view of guests across the table, which will make conversation difficult.

• The last point to remember is that even the most experienced hosts occasionally have the odd disaster, but the secret is to remain calm! As a last resort it is sensible to keep a standby meal in the freezer which can be used in an emergency. This will save the embarrassment of having to tell your guests that they will not be eating as there was slight mishap in the kitchen, or of having to phone for a pizza to be delivered.

Handy Housework Hints

Does anybody really enjoy housework? If you answered yes to this question then you are in a strange minority: for most people it is a chore that they could well do without. If you are one of the lucky ones you might have your own cleaner, but there will be still be many cleaning jobs that you will have to do yourself. There are normally one or two areas of cleaning that a person finds really horrible, for instance cleaning the oven. The following section does not promise to make cleaning enjoyable but it should make it less of a burden.

There are further cleaning tips in the section on spring cleaning.

Top tips:
● Before cleaning, change into an old pair of clothes: a splash of bleach is all that it takes to ruin a garment.

● It is more efficient to clean one room thoroughly than several superficially.

● Buy a plastic box with a handle that you can keep all your cleaning equipment in. This saves trying to carry armfuls of cleaning agents and cloths. If you want to be really sensible have two separate boxes, one downstairs and one upstairs. Then wherever you are you will never be far away from a duster.

● Try to get into a methodical routine, one in which you clean on a regular day each week rather than just trying to fit it in when you feel like it.

● Wash dusters and cleaning cloths on a regular basis. There is no point cleaning with a cloth that is in more need of cleaning than the surface you are about to clean.

● When hoovering, avoid picking up any sharp metal objects that might rip the bag.

Anti-static
If you have ever had one of those visitors that surreptitiously inspect your home for signs of dust and dirt, you will know how embarrassing it can be when it is pointed out that there are cobwebs and dust everywhere.

• Certain household objects act as magnets to dust and can build up a thick layer in a matter of days, such as televisions, video recorders and home computers: this is due to the static electricity they generate. It will help reduce the dust if you spray them with an anti-static spray. These are suitable for a number of surfaces that attract dust, but check the instructions before using.

Baths

The British take more baths than any other European country, in fact people in many countries regard baths as unhygienic due to the fact you are sitting in dirty water. I can't see what all the fuss is about: I can think of nothing better than relaxing in a bath with a drink in hand after a hard day's work.

The problem with baths is that they can get dirty. If you have sporty members of your household who play rugby or a similar game then you will know exactly what I mean. To help, keep a cloth and bath cleaner in the bathroom so that whoever last used the bath cleans it afterwards. This might take some nagging!

• To remove rust stains from an enamel bath scrub with half a lemon. If this fails try a 10% solution of hydrochloric acid. The rust stains would be caused as a result of a dripping trap, so to stop the stains from recurring fit a new washer.

Brass

• If the brass is stained it can be tackled using a solution of 2 tablespoons of vinegar and 1 of salt, then wash off and finish with a brass polish.

Bread Bins

• Clean these regularly as crumbs can build up and go mouldy producing a foul smell and making your fresh bread go off.

Cane furniture

• Cane furniture can be cleaned using a household cream cleaner on a soft cloth. Wipe off using a damp cloth. It is important that the furniture should not get too wet.

• If the furniture is varnished but is looking a little shabby, then give it a couple of coats of varnish.

Carpets

Carpets are still the most popular form of floor covering in this country and there is a vast range to choose from. Carpets are made from a variety of fabrics including wool, acrylic, polyester, cotton, viscose rayon, and polypropylene. Sometimes blends are produced to reduce the cost and increase durability.

When choosing a carpet there are a number of factors to be considered...

• Is a carpet the most sensible choice of floor covering? Eg. a carpet in a kitchen will soon look shabby. A surface that can be cleaned easily is the most sensible choice.

• If you are planning on moving after a year or two it is not worth going to great expense when buying a carpet because when you come to sell you will not be able to take it with you and you will receive little of the original cost from the new buyer.

• Certain areas in the house are subject to more wear and tear than others: areas such as the stairs and the hall are put under the most stress. When choosing a carpet, think about whether it is going to be heavily used.

• The better the quality of the carpet the more likely it is to last. If you are planning on staying in the same house for a long time then it makes sense to buy a hard wearing carpet. It is a false economy to buy a cheap one, as it could mean that you have to replace it after a few years, which means paying twice in total.

• If you have children or young pets you might want to consider having a stain proof carpet, as both children and puppies specialise in messing up carpets.

• It is advisable to wash your carpets once a year to stop them from getting shabby. When you have a new carpet fitted make sure you remember to keep a piece as a sample. It is useful to have a piece of the carpet you can use as a tester for stain removal and to take with you when you are shopping for wallpaper and other furnishings. In the case of a major disaster on the carpet, such as an iron burn, the affected area can be cut out and replaced with the spare section. This is only to be done as a last resort because the join will nearly always show.

• If you decide to rearrange the furniture in a room, you will find that where heavy pieces have been there are dents in the carpet where the legs have squashed the pile. These can look unsightly especially if the carpet is deep, and although the 'dents' will eventually go, it can take many months. To remove the dents place a wet towel that has been folded twice over the area and steam with a hot iron.

Chamois Leather

Chamois leathers are produced either from sheep or goats and they have a natural capacity to absorb water effectively. This makes them extremely useful for drying large wet areas such as cars after they have been washed. A decent chamois leather is not cheap, and unless they are properly looked after they will soon deteriorate. After use they should be wrung out gently and lightly stretched occasionally so they keep their shape. If a chamois is left unattended it will dry rigidly and be useless.

Cobwebs

If you have high ceilings and find it difficult to reach cobwebs in these parts, tie a duster to the top of a household broom. This will save you getting up on a chair which you have to move around the room as you clean. Alternatively, if your Hoover has a long enough arm, simply suck up the cobwebs straight into the machine.

Cooker cleaning

This is normally rated as one of the most hated of all cleaning jobs: the interior of an oven builds up a disgusting layer of grease, and if you cook a lot of roast dinners it will be even worse. Unfortunately, the longer it is left the harder the task will be when you do come to deal with it.

• Remember to give the door of the oven a wipe every time you use it, as this will stop the build up of grease. If you don't remember or just can't be bothered, try a specialised oven cleaner, making sure that you read the instructions carefully because some of these cleaners are very strong and can cause harm if they come into contact with the skin or eyes. Even if you wear rubber gloves, as often recommended, bare skin on the upper arm sometimes comes into contact with the cleaning substance when reaching deep into the oven, and this can cause adverse reactions and burns, so wear an old top with long sleeves.

• It is also good practice to wipe down the top of the cooker each time it is used. This should prevent your cooker from ever getting to that stage where it would be more suited for use in a student kitchen (students only clean cookers when the grime has built up to such an extent that the hobs are no longer visible and the griddle pan is a lake of fat and grease).

• If something boils over in the oven or on the hobs, deal with it immediately if it is safe to do so. You can either try to wipe it quickly with a cloth, but there is the risk that you might burn yourself, or you can sprinkle a thick layer of salt over the spillage and clean it up when the surface has cooled.

Copper

The problem with copper is that it builds up tarnish very quickly so if you have a large number of copper objects you will be kept busy. Although copper does not rust it is susceptible to a green deposit called verdigris. To remove this deposit clean with a cloth impregnated with methylated spirit and powdered chalk. To polish copper use a special copper polish.

Curtains

Don't forget to hoover your curtains gently once in a while as it is amazing how dusty they can get. When it comes to washing curtains the utmost care should be taken: if your curtains are very old or particularly thin, it is better to hand-wash them, if they are washed in a machine they might well fall apart.

Door mats

If your carpets are constantly having muddy footprints on them, you either do not have a door mat or it is not being used. Door mats are essential to stop mud and dirt being transferred on to your carpets, so stick them at the front and back doors. If you want to keep your carpets really clean instigate a 'leave the shoes at the door' policy, and you will be amazed at how much cleaner your carpets stay. You also don't have the worry of certain unwanted types of dirt being trodden into your carpet.

Dustbins

Although Britain is regarded as a nation of animal lovers, if your dustbin has ever been ransacked by hungry animals and the contents strewn around the garden you might feel a little less good natured towards them. Make sure that you have a dustbin that has a secure lid, the ones with the clamps are the best, and remember, always wrap up any food that is being thrown away. Animals can smell a portion of unwanted casserole a mile away! If you are still having problems put a few drops of ammonia in the dustbin, as animals find this most unpleasant and it should ward them off.

Electric Food Mixers (and Processors)

After making a cake there is the arduous task of washing up the mixer or processor, depending on what was used. Here are a couple of tips to help with the cleaning:

• Using a spatula, scrape out as much of the mixture as possible, then switch the machine on again for a brief moment. This should get rid of the mixture that has stuck to the blades. Use the spatula again to remove the residue.

• After removing the mixture pour in some hot water with a little washing up liquid, then switch on, and it should clean itself.

Finger Marks

Certain places such as light switches and doors suffer from grubby finger marks, and if you have young children the problem will be even worse. It is amazing what they manage to transfer from the table to other parts of the house via their fingers. One of the best ways of removing finger marks is to use a little methylated spirit on a cloth: this is an effective agent on greasy marks.

Floors

Whatever type your floors are, be they Formica, ceramic tiles, wood or vinyl, they all need to be looked after. Floors should be swept on a regular basis to stop the build up of any dirt, and this makes it easier when it comes to washing or polishing the floor. Each surface will require a different cleaner. Wooden floors with a wax finish are time consuming to maintain, and they need a good layer of wax for protection so it is essential they are not neglected.

Glass

If you don't have any glass cleaner then make your own from a mixture of vinegar and water.

Hairbrushes

It is only natural bristle brushes that are difficult to clean. First of all, using a comb remove as much of the hair as possible, then dip the bristles in a solution of baking soda and water. It is important that only the bristles come into contact with the solution. When the bristles look clean rinse with water.

Irons

Unless you keep the soleplate of your iron clean you will find that you begin to get marks appearing on your clothes. If you burn a fabric it will normally stick to the soleplate making the iron unusable. To clean, turn the iron off then scrape off as much as you can with a knife and then use a proprietary iron cleaner.

Jewellery

If you are in doubt as to the value of any of your jewellery then take it along to a jeweller for a valuation. Do the same if you are unsure what material an item is made out of. It is possible to buy special jewellery cleaning kits, but generally everyday cleaning products can be used. Hard stones such as diamonds can be cleaned with a little washing up liquid and then rinsed and dried. Soft stones should be cleaned with a chamois cloth, as should pearls.

Not only is most jewellery valuable, it normally has a sentimental attachment as well. If you see that a stone is coming loose from a piece stop wearing it and have it mended, also if a ring is loose then have it adjusted. You may find it hard to forgive yourself if you lose it.

Kettles

If you live in an area with hard water you will suffer from limescale. It causes a number of problems: kettles are prone to furring up with limescale deposits, and this makes the kettle less efficient and will cost more to run. Another problem caused by limescale is the froth that can be produced after boiling. This leaves a horrible scum on the surface of a drink. To avoid this, descale your kettle regularly using a special kettle descaling agent. If you want to prevent your kettle from furring up so quickly, fill the kettle using water that has been filtered or try placing a marble in the bottom of the kettle. If you still have a problem with froth, use a tea strainer when pouring water from the kettle, which should stop the froth ending up in your drink.

Mattresses

Turn mattresses over every few months. This helps to stop them from wearing in one particular place. Use an old blanket to put between the mattress and the bottom sheet to help protect the mattress from any stains. For children it is advisable to put a plastic sheet underneath.

Pewter

Produced from an alloy of tin and lead it can be used to make a variety of objects, although it cannot be used in cooking as the heat will cause the metal to melt. Pewter, like most metals must be cleaned and polished on a regular basis to stop it from corroding. Pewter can be cleaned either with a proprietary pewter polish or a mixture of whiting and oil.

Silver

Whether your silver is plate or solid it will require loving attention as they are both subject to tarnishing, but the effort will be worth it. If the silver is suffering from corrosion a proprietary silver dip can be used, but wash the silver after removing from the dip. With silver plate that is wearing a little thin do not leave in the dip for very long. After removing the tarnish use a proprietary silver polish.

Do-It-Yourself

The following chapter is not intended as a guide to how to undertake major DIY projects. Its main objective is to give a few tips and tricks of the trade to aid the most common DIY exploits.

Here are a few golden rules:

- Never undertake a job which you can't handle, either through a lack of experience or time.

- Always read up on the project that you intend to undertake.

- Remember that a badly done job will only have to be redone, or it could be unsafe and cause an accident.

- Never take short cuts.

- Seek guidance from an expert if you are having difficulties.

- Never take risks, especially when fitting electrical items, or when using power tools.

- Make sure that what you intend to do is legal, ie. planning permission may be needed for certain DIY projects.

- Have the proper tools for the job.

- Use the recommended materials.

- Good luck!

Electrical

There are a number of small electrical jobs that a DIY enthusiast can undertake if they have adequate knowledge. However, as with most DIY projects, especially those of an electrical nature, never attempt a job that should be left to a qualified electrician. Dabbling with household wiring or electrical appliances is particularly hazardous (see section on electrical safety).

It is amazing how many people are still unsure how to wire a plug correctly. Fortunately, most appliances that are now purchased come fitted with a plug. Ask the retailer to fit the plug if one is not already attached: otherwise they are selling you an incomplete product! If you have to fit the plug yourself, pay attention to the instruction printed either on the plug itself or on a label attached to the flex.

If you have to replace the flex on an electrical appliance make sure you become familiar with the correct wiring procedure. Since the 1970s the colour-coding of wires has been standardised so they are now the same throughout Europe.

Some older appliances may still be wired with the old colour coding.

Wiring of old appliances

Green	=	Earth
Red	=	Live
Black	=	Neutral

Wiring of new appliances

Green / Yellow =   Earth
Brown   =   Live
Blue   =   Neutral

Keep a small electrical tool kit in an easy to find place in the house. It is useful to be able to find fuses and a torch quickly when needed.

Electrical tips:

• Never overload sockets with too many plugs, especially if they are running appliances that draw a large current as this can be hazardous.

• Dust light bulbs. If a layer of dust accumulates they can overheat.

• Extension leads should only be used as a temporary measure. They are not designed for permanent use. If you use one on a spool make sure that it is fully unwound before use, as they can overheat if they are used when still coiled up.

• Make sure that you don't use an extension lead for any appliances that draw large currents, or at least check that it is safe before using.

Fuses

The fuse is a simple but effective invention. A fuse is a small piece of metal with a low melting point. If there is a problem with the electrics and they begin to overheat the fuse will blow because it has a lower melting point than the rest of the wiring. This breaks the electrical circuit, rendering it safe.

Electric circuits contain a fuse to protect the wiring and appliances. Without a fuse there would be a risk of damage, including fire. A common cause of a blown fuse is when an electric appliance that draws a heavy current is plugged into a circuit that is only designed for a lighter current.

● If an electric circuit stops working find the fuse box, check the fuses and replace if necessary. Before removing any fuses turn the electricity off at the mains.

● A house will normally have a central fuse box.

There are three basic types of fuses.

● The most common type of fuse works by a piece of wire being placed across a insulated porcelain or bakelite fuse carrier. It is easy to see if the wire is broken and a new piece of fuse wire can be fitted.

Protected fuse
This is similar to the above, except that the wire is protected which makes it harder to see if it has blown. To check, remove the wire from one end.

Cartridge fuse
These use a slightly more modern design and are easier to fit as the fuse wire is encased in a cartridge (similar to a standard plug fuse).

Some electric systems are now fitted with their own circuit breaker which cuts in and terminates the power supply. There is no fuse, and the circuit can be reset when the problem has been rectified.

• If a fuse blows repeatedly then seek assistance from an electrician.

Plug fuses
Electrical appliances are fitted with cartridge fuses which will blow if there is a short circuit with the wiring or an overload. The fuse is there to safeguard the appliance to which it is fitted, and when an appliance stops working a blown fuse is the most likely cause.

• Appliances are normally fitted with between a 3-amp or a 13-amp fuse depending on the application. Appliances such as radios, clocks, tape recorders and lamps should normally be fitted with a 3-amp fuse.

• 13-amp fuses should be used with appliances such as electric heaters, freezers, fridges and Hoovers.

• If you are uncertain which fuse should be fitted, consult the manual or contact the manufacturer for advice.

Painting
The following tips are for painting in the decorating sense of the word. Sorry if you aspire to be the next Picasso.

• Always use the correct paint for the job, ie. emulsion is not suitable for paintwork, and special paints are needed for exterior work. There is a wide choice of paints available giving a variety of finishes, so when purchasing paint, check that you have picked up the right finish.

• Always use dust sheets to protect other surfaces from splashes of paint, because however careful you may be it is almost impossible not to make a mess. Although it is time consuming, protecting surfaces is worthwhile, as you will spend twice as long cleaning up if you don't bother.

• Prepare surfaces that are about to be painted. Remove all traces of dirt, cobwebs, grease and rust then wash down with warm soapy water. If you are about to paint over a gloss surface, rub it down first with a medium grade sandpaper and then wash.

• Treat any wood knots in new wood with a specific wood sealer.

• Instead of trying to mask small items which are fiddly, cover them in a coating of Vaseline. After painting this can be wiped off.

• Any paint that is accidentally left on windows whilst painting can be removed in a number of ways. One is to use turpentine, or a solution of warm water and vinegar (3:1 ratio). Try to remove any unwanted paint as quickly as possible: the longer it is there the harder it will be to remove. It is advisable to mask the window frames to avoid this happening.

• If you are using a coloured paint try to keep some paint spare and don't throw the tin away as you might need it in the future to repair any scrapes. Although it might be possible to buy the paint used, if you have thrown the tin away it is a waste of money to buy a new tin just for a few touch ups.

● Another reason for keeping a small amount is that if you buy a new tin some time later the colour might have changed slightly or you may have forgotten the brand of paint you originally used.

● The most effective way of keeping paint from drying out is to make sure the lid is on as tightly as possible. If you have trouble getting the lid on, use a small block of wood and tap gently with a hammer, then wrap the tin in foil.

● If you are unsure what colour you are going to use, purchase a tester size of the paint, then paint the back of an old piece of wallpaper and hang it up to give you an idea what it will look like.

● When painting up a ladder, pour some of the paint into a smaller receptacle. It will be easier to work with, and if you drop the paint it will not make so much mess.

● Mask light switches and wall sockets to avoid getting paint on them.

● If you always manage to drip paint off your brush, however hard you try not to, here is a solution. Using a paper plate push the handle of the brush through the centre of plate so the plate catches the drips instead of your hand.

● White spirit can be re-used if it was used previously for cleaning gloss paint from brushes. How? Easy, the residue that is left after cleaning the brushes will sink to the bottom of the jar and will leave a clean solution of white spirit.

• It is always worthwhile buying the best quality paint brushes you can afford. The less expensive brushes have a bad habit of depositing their bristles on your freshly painted surface. A well made brush will last for years if looked after.

• After cleaning a brush thoroughly, wrap it in newspaper or foil and lie flat.

• If when you come to use your brush you find that it is stiff, don't throw it away: there is a solution. Heat some vinegar in an old saucepan, don't let it quite boil, then place the brush in vinegar for a couple of minutes. Rinse before using.

Painting interiors
Before starting the painting the first thing to do is the planning and the preparation of the surfaces.

• This involves choosing the paint, the type, the colour and calculating how much you require. If you are unsure of the colour you want and whether it will look right, you can buy testers. These are small quantities of the paint, that enable you to paint a small area to see if you like it before going ahead and buying a large quantity.

• Make sure that you have clean brushes, brush cleaner, masking tape, sandpaper, rags, fillers for both wood and wall, paint stripper and plenty of old sheets.

• Prepare the room you are going to be painting. Painting can be a messy business, so don't take any chances. Clear away any furniture, remove curtains etc. that could be in the line of drips and splashes and cover other surfaces with dust sheets. If you don't you will be surprised, even if you take the utmost care, how far paint can travel. You should also protect yourself, wear old clothes that are disposable and if you are like me and always get paint in your hair when painting the ceiling, try wearing an old cap or even a handkerchief.

• Prepare the surfaces. Don't be tempted to cut corners by going straight into the painting, because the surfaces could be dirty, greasy (especially in the kitchen), or dusty. All surfaces must be washed with sugar soap, then wiped down with clean water.

• If there are any cracks in plasterwork, they must be repaired first. Remove any loose plaster and use filler (you will have to wait for the filler to dry before you commence with the painting of that area). If there are any large holes they will need plastering, which is really a job for a professional.

• With woodwork, it can either be rubbed down with fine sandpaper if the paintwork is in good condition, or if the woodwork is in poor condition the surface will need stripping down to the bare wood. Remove any rotten wood and treat, then you will need a coat of primer, undercoat and a top coat.

• If you are planning on painting a whole room it is usual to start with the ceiling, then the walls and finally the woodwork. Make sure that you choose the right size brush for the job: if you try to use a large brush for intricate work such as window frames you will find that you get more paint on the window than you do on the frame.

• When painting the skirting boards place a piece of card between the board and the floor. This will protect the surface and make it much easier to paint.

• When painting do not put too much paint on the brush as it will result in runs in the paintwork and will probably drip onto the floor. You will get a better finish if you use two thin coats as opposed to one thick one.

More DIY Tips

• When using a hammer to remove nails from delicate wood, put a thin piece of wood under the head of the hammer to protect the wood form getting marked or dented.

• If you have to nail two pieces of wood together and one is thinner than the other, make sure that you nail through the thin piece into the thicker.

• If you seem to hit your thumb more times than you hit the nail when hammering, try pushing the nail through a piece of thin card: it is then possible to hold the card instead of holding the nail. When the nail is in sufficiently the card can be gently pulled away from the nail.

• If you are using small nails, use a small pin hammer. This will lessen the chance of breaking the nail or hitting your thumb.

Sawing

• Any saw used should be sharp and free from rust.

• Choose the most appropriate saw for the job - it is no good trying to cut balsa wood with a chain saw!

• Don't force the saw when cutting.

• Never use a wood saw for cutting metal, it will ruin the teeth of the saw.

• To make sawing easier, clamp small pieces of wood, and when cutting logs use a workbench or saw horse.

• When cutting heavy wood make sure that the waste piece of wood is supported as it might break off causing the wood to splinter, possibly ruining both pieces of wood.

• Always remember to cut on the waste side of the line you have marked. If you cut through the line you have drawn it will not be accurate, because of the thickness of the blade.

Wallpapering
Wallpapering is more expensive than painting and is more time consuming, but it can give a room a warm feeling that cannot be achieved by painting. The following are a few basic tips to get you started. Consult a specialist DIY book for more help.

What you will need:
• Bucket
• Decorator's scissors
• Large paste brush
• Pencil
• Plumb line
• Pasting table
• Craft knife for trimming edges

Estimating

● A standard roll of British wallpaper is 10.05m long by 0.53m wide and will cover an area of 5 square metres. Some continental wallpapers are slightly narrower.

● Use a manufacturer's chart to calculate how many rolls of wallpaper will be required.

● Always buy slightly more paper than is exactly needed, this is to allow for mistakes and to account for pattern matching.

The wallpaper

There are numerous types of wallpaper, each giving a different finish and effect. There are certain wallpapers such as ones produced from vinyl that can be washed down: these are sensible if you have children, or for use in bathrooms. They require a special paste that contains a fungicide.

● When choosing wallpaper take home a sample so you can get an idea what it will look like.

● Check that all rolls are from the same batch, as there might be slight variations in colour between batches. If you have not bought enough, then by the time you realise that you need some more the original batch may have sold out.

● The thicker the wallpaper the easier it is to hang. It will also cover any blemishes in a wall better than a thinner paper. If your wall is in very bad shape and you can't afford to have it replastered use a textured paper.

• Cheap thin papers are prone to tearing and have a habit of fading, so in the long run try to buy the best quality you can afford. It could save you money over a long period of time.

• Always use a specially designed wallpaper for areas that are susceptible to damp or condensation eg. bathrooms or kitchens.

Adhesives
Always use the recommended paste for the type of wallpaper you are using, and mix it according to the instructions. Never be tempted to use more paste than is recommended.

Preparation
As when painting, preparation is the secret to a good finish.

• Papering over existing wallpaper is not recommended, as the paste from the new wallpaper might cause the old paper to lift from the wall, and if this occurs you will have to start over again.

• To remove old wallpaper, soak small areas of wallpaper with warm water, leave for a few minutes for the water to soak in and then remove with a scraper. Before soaking the walls, remember to protect the floor from any water that may be spilt.

• Never use a sharp edged tool as there is a risk of gouging the plaster.

• After removing old wallpaper wash down walls and fill in any cracks in the plaster with wall filler.

More top tips

● If after wallpapering there are bubbles that cannot be smoothed out, try injecting a small quantity of paste into the area using a syringe, wait a few minutes then smooth out with a cloth.

● If you have young children it is advisable to purchase a washable wallpaper, so grubby marks can be removed easily.

Plumbing
Sinks, baths, and basins are all prone to the occasional blockage of the waste pipe. Even a partial blockage can mean that it takes longer for the water to drain away and can lead to a total blockage.

Blocked sink

● The most effective way of unblocking a pipe is to use a plunger, which can be purchased from a DIY shop. A plunger is normally made from a rubber hemisphere with a wooden handle.

● Before using the plunger block up the overflow with a rag, then place the rubber part over the waste outlet. Push the wooden handle of the plunger down and up with a degree of force. This should hopefully shift the blockage.

● *If this fails try poking a wire coat-hanger down to free whatever is blocking it. If you are still having no luck then the problem is probably in the U bend pipe. There is normally an access cap at the base of the pipe that can be removed, but place a bowl underneath to catch the water. When all the water has drained away use a piece of wire to prod around to see if you can remove the obstruction.*

Blocked drains

There are two indicators of a blocked drain. The first can sometimes be seen in the toilet where the water level will be higher than normal after flushing. The other sign could be water overflowing from a gully or manhole. Clearing drains can be a messy business, so before you start put your old clothes on.

● The first thing to do is work out where the blockage is. This can be done by removing the manhole covers on your property and seeing which ones are flooded. From this information it can be deduced where the blockage lies.

• To remove a blockage requires the use of drain rods which can be hired from tool hire shops. After screwing the rods together push the rod in the direction of the blockage up the half channel. The rods will come with a variety of accessories that can be fitted on to the end of the rod. Once the rod comes into contact with the blockage it will normally dislodge it and the water in the manhole will clear.

• After the blockage has been cleared run the taps for a while to clear any remaining debris, then flush the area with warm soapy water.

Burst pipes

• When faced with a burst pipe the first thing to do is to find a container to catch the water that is leaking from the pipe, then shut off the water supply to prevent flooding.

• When all the water is mopped up, call a plumber to come and fix the pipe.

Frozen pipes

If you have a frozen pipe there is a chance that the pipe may crack as the water inside the pipe expands. Check the pipe carefully for signs of any ice where the pipe might have burst. If there is no indication of damage the pipe can be thawed, either by wrapping cloths soaked in hot water around the pipe or by using a hairdryer. If there are signs of damage have the pipe repaired before attempting to thaw it.

Condensation

Condensation is produced when moisture suspended in warm air comes into contact with a cold surface such as a window pane. Condensation can occur on many other surfaces such as on walls, ceilings, mirrors and floors.

The effects of condensation can be to cause paint to peel, wallpaper to bubble, and it can also increase the spread of mould and mildew.

If you suffer from a condensation problem the solution is to remove the damp air before it does any harm. The most effective way of removing the air is to use an extractor fan. These should be fitted in bathrooms and kitchens as these are usually the worst spots. If you can't afford to have fans fitted, open a window when you are using the kitchen or bathroom.

The other alternative is to buy a special machine that stops condensation from forming. Even cheaper than this is a device that uses crystals to extract moisture from the atmosphere and collect it in a container. They only cost a few pounds and can extract as much a half a pint of water from the air in a damp room in a day!

Doors

The main problems with doors are sticking or squeaking, and both can be a source of annoyance.

If a door is difficult to close it could be due to three possible causes: swelling, sagging or sticking.

Swelling
External wooden doors are prone to changing shape according to the time of year. In the winter a door will swell due to the damp wet weather, then in the summer they shrink when they dry out. When a door swells it might be difficult to open and close. The cure is to plane the swollen edges, making sure that you don't plane too much off otherwise in the summer there will be a draughty gap.

Sagging
If the screws that hold the hinge to the door frame become loose the door could sag under the weight. Tighten up the screws, and if need be fit longer screws.

Squeaking
This is a very common problem and if you have the cobwebs to accompany it, it can give your house the haunted effect. To cure a squeaking door work a little oil or spray some WD40 into the hinges and then open and shut the door a few times.

Stain Removal

How many times have you been in the situation where you have just put on a clean shirt or jumper then seconds later you end up spilling a drink or food all down yourself? What do you do: panic, or keep calm and remove the stain by the most appropriate method? Panic doesn't remove stains!

Carpets, clothes and upholstery are most likely to suffer from stain abuse, but other surfaces such as wood, floor tiles and objects are not exempt from unwanted deposits.

Before coming to the advice on removing stains, some consideration must be given to avoiding stains in the first place. In theory most of them are caused by carelessness: that coffee cup left on the floor that you meant to pick up but didn't is symbolic of the most common type of culprit. Drinks should be left on level surfaces, off the floor, and not too close to the edge. Make plenty of clear space for glasses at parties so that people don't have to put them on the floor or the stereo etc. Don't bring your best clothes into contact with your messiest hobbies, such as gardening, DIY or spaghetti eating.

When a stain occurs prompt action is essential: if you take immediate action you are more likely to be successful in removing the stain than if you leave it for a while. Here are a few simple guide-lines that should be followed:

• Check whether the fabric with the spillage is washable or not. If the item is not washable it will require different treatment, so follow the instructions on the label.

• Have a 'stain kit' that you can access quickly when required, comprising of clean cloths, paper towels and sponges to soak up any spillage. This will save hunting through cupboards for the appropriate cleaning agents and clean rags.

• Make sure that if you are using a chemical agent on a fabric that it will not damage the fabric. Pay particular attention to fabrics that have been specially coated, eg. flame resistant materials. Hydrogen peroxide should never be used on nylon.

● There is a potential hazard involved in using some cleaning chemicals. Read the instructions before use and ensure that you have adequate ventilation when using them.

● Keep cleaning materials out of the reach of young children as they could prove fatal if they are swallowed or inhaled or cause burns to the skin.

● Before trying to remove a stain on a colour fabric, test that the fabric is colourfast by choosing a part of the item where it will not show. If the colour runs do not try any further attempts to remove the stain and take it to a dry cleaner.

● The most effective way to remove a stain is to tackle the stain from the back of the garment with a cloth on the other side to absorb the spilt substance. If you do it in this way you are not pushing the stain through the surface of the fabric, you are hopefully taking it back the way it came.

● Never assume that hot water is the best method of washing stains: it could cause the stain to set in, making it harder to remove in the future. Play it safe and use warm or cold water unless you are sure that hot water is the most effective temperature to use.

● When removing a stain, change to a clean cloth as soon as it becomes stained, as you will not be doing any good if you are using a dirty cloth.

● If you think that you will be unable to remove the stain and will take the garment to a dry cleaner, don't make any attempts at trying to remove the stain, just inform the dry cleaner of the nature of the problem.

Common stain removers and cleaning agents

Ammonia - you can't miss the smell: it is quite pungent, but it is nevertheless a useful cleaning agent. It should be used in a diluted form, normally one part ammonia to four parts water. It can cause irritation and burns to the skin if care is not taken.

Biological detergents - many washing powders are now available without any biological enzymes, but it is still possible to buy both. A biological detergent is more efficient at removing certain stains, such as those that are protein based, eg. blood and milk.

Bleach - this is a powerful agent that has a number of uses, not only for cleaning. Bleach should only be used on white items such as cotton, never on delicate items. Undiluted bleach is not normally used in stain removal as it can do more damage than good. It should be diluted according to the strength required: if it is a small stain then use 10 ml per litre of water. If you are going to soak the item you need to use the same amount of bleach, but add up to ten litres of water. Make sure that when you have finished using the bleach that you rinse the garment thoroughly, because if you don't the bleach may continue working.

Borax - this has a mild bleaching effect and is particularly useful on acid-based stains, such as fruit stains. Use roughly two teaspoons of borax to half a litre of warm water and soak the item for 10 to 15 minutes.

Glycerine - this is not so useful for removing new stains, but can be used to loosen an old stain. Dilute with water in equal parts.

Hydrogen peroxide - this is also a type of bleaching agent, but is not as strong as standard bleach. As it is not so powerful it is more suitable for use on delicate garments where you would not use standard bleach, such as thin cottons, silks and wool. There are certain fabrics that it should not be used on, such as nylon. Dilute with water to a ratio of six parts water to one part hydrogen peroxide.

Jeweller's Rouge - this is a fine red powder which is mildly abrasive and is used for cleaning silver.

Lemon juice - its natural acidic properties make it an ideal cleaner, it can be used to remove iron mould and marks from marble.

Methylated spirit - this has a number of uses including stain removal. It is used undiluted: pour a little on a cloth and test on a hidden part of the garment before use.

Salt - this works well on soaking up stains such as red wine, and is also effective at removing blood stains.

Vinegar (white) - mixed with water or used on its own it is a very effective and cheap cleaning agent.

Washing-up liquid - this is normally close at hand when a stain occurs and is surprisingly effective when used with warm water on carpets. Don't oversoak and only use a little washing up liquid. Rinse with clean water afterwards.

There are a number of specifically manufactured cleaning products that are useful for dealing with even the toughest stains.

A-Z of stains

Acids
Washable items
Place the garment under cold running water, then remove and using a solution of borax and warm water try to remove the acid. Then rinse in clean water. Take care when cleaning acids that you do not get any acid on your skin, rinse immediately with lots of water if you do. If the acid is particularly strong, such as battery acid, it may have ruined the garment even before you have had a chance to remove it.

Non-washable items
Normally a lost cause.

Adhesives
There are many different adhesives and each type can require a separate method of removal. Some are easy to remove such as latex glue but others can be more troublesome.

Adhesive tape
Washable items
Remove any residue with methylated spirit.

Non-washable items
As above.

Adhesives - animal or fish-based glues
Washable items
These are fairly easy to remove. Wash in cold water, if this does not work then use a biological powder.

Non-washable items
Sponge with cold water with and a little detergent.

Adhesives - contact adhesives
Washable items
Either use nail varnish or acetone, except on items produced from acetate. Then wash as normal.

Non-washable items
As above, but do not wash. If a mark remains take to a dry cleaner.

Adhesives - clear adhesives
Washable items
Either use nail varnish or acetone, except on items produced from acetate. Then wash as normal.

Non-washable items
As above, but do not wash. If a mark remains take to a dry cleaner.

Epoxy adhesives
Washable items
It is essential that you try to remove this type of glue before it sets because it is almost impossible to remove otherwise. If the glue is not hard try methylated spirit or cellulose thinners.

Non-washable items
As above.

Latex adhesives
Washable and non-washable items
This type of glue can be removed with cold water and a cloth. If there is any glue that is left after the garment has dried it should just peel off using your fingers.

Alcohol - beer
Washable items
Sponge off any residue and then wash in the usual way with a biological powder.

Non-washable items
Try to mop up as much as possible using something like kitchen paper and then sponge out with warm water.

Alcohol - spirits
Washable items
Treat with the same method as for beer.

Non-washable items
Soak up any residue then sponge with warm water and a little liquid detergent, or alternatively use a small amount of methylated spirit on a cloth.

Alcohol - wine
Washable items
Cover the stain with a liberal sprinkling of salt and then soak in cold water before washing.

Non-washable items
Talcum powder is the most effective way to blot up the wine, then sponge off with clean warm water.

Bird droppings
Washable items
Remove any residual mess then soak in cold water with a little biological powder, then wash as usual.

Non-washable items
Remove any residual mess then clean using a mixture of ammonia and water, with 6 parts water to 1 part ammonia, then dab with white vinegar.

Blood
Washables
Soak at once in a strong solution of salt and water and leave for five to ten minutes, then change the solution and repeat the process. Make sure that you do not rub stained wool. Run it under cold water and then rinse several times with salt water.

Non-washable items

Blot up as much as possible then sponge the spot with a solution of water with a few drops of ammonia in it. Then rinse with cold water and blot dry.

Candle wax
Washable items

Try to put the garment in the freezer so the wax hardens; it can then be scraped off more easily. If there are any traces left, put the affected area between two pieces of blotting paper and iron on a low setting. The wax should be absorbed by the blotting paper. To finish off use a dry cleaning agent or methylated spirit.

Carbon Paper
Washable items

Use undiluted liquid detergent, then a small amount of ammonia. Rinse well.

Non-washable items

Use methylated spirit on a piece of sponge. If this fails, take to a dry cleaner.

Chewing Gum
Washable items

Scrape off what you can then put the garment in the freezer for about an hour. After this it should come off easily. If there is any left then try putting the affected area between two sheets of brown paper and gently iron. One last trick is to apply egg white before washing.

Non-washable items
Use the freezing technique, if this fails try a little methylated spirit. If the gum is on a carpet or upholstery try placing ice cubes on the area, then use methylated spirit.

Chocolate
Washable items
Remove any residue, then sponge the area with a solution of borax or soapy water. Wash with a biological detergent.

Non-washable items
Remove any residue, then take to the dry cleaner.

Coffee
Washable items
Soak in a bowl of water with a biological detergent. If it is stubborn leave to soak overnight.

Non-washable items
Blot up as much as is possible with paper towels, then sponge with a solution of borax.

Crayon
Small children have a habit of drawing on walls with crayons. The best way to remove the marks is to use a cloth with a little lighter fuel.

Cream
Washable items

Remove as much as possible, then soak in cool water, then wash with a biological detergent. If there is still a mark use a proprietary grease solvent.

Non-washable items
After sponging off any residue, treat with a proprietary grease solvent or take to a dry cleaner.

Curry
Washable items
Soak in warm water, then scrub with a solution of water and glycerine in equal parts. After scrubbing rinse and wash with a biological powder.

Non-washable items
Remove any residue, then sponge with a solution of borax and warm water.

Deodorants
Washable items
Before washing with a biological powder try applying a paste of salt and bicarbonate of soda, which is rubbed into the area and left for 20 minutes.

Non-washable items
Take to a dry cleaner.

Dye
Washable items
If the stain is small try to remove as much as possible by blotting up with a paper towel, then sponge with cold water. If the stain is large then soak in cold water with a biological detergent.

Non-washable items
Take to a dry cleaner as soon as possible.

Egg
Washable items
Remove any remnants of egg and if it is still runny soak in cold water, then wash with a biological powder.

Non-washable items
Remove any excess, then use a proprietary grease solvent.

Fruit stains
Washable items
Rinse in cold water, then stretch the item over the top of a pan and pour hot water over the stain. Wash as normal.

Non-washable items
Sponge out as much as possible, then take to a dry cleaner.

Grass
Washable items
Dab the area with methylated spirit and then wash with biological powder.

Non-washable items
Make a paste, using equal quantities of salt and cream of tartar and a little water and rub into the stain. When it is dry brush out the paste gently with a brush.

Gravy
Washable items
Use cold water and a little detergent, if this doesn't shift the stain use a proprietary grease solvent.

Non-washable items
Sponge off as much as possible using cold soapy water, then use a proprietary grease solvent.

Grease
Washable items
Dust talcum powder over a grease stain to prevent the stain from spreading and to absorb some of the grease. Then use a dry cleaning agent, and finally wash as normal.

Non-washable items
Send to a dry cleaner.

Ink - ball point
Washable items
Sponge with warm water and liquid detergent then wash as normal. If there is any sign of a stain still present, use a little nail polish remover (must not be used on acetate).

Non-washable items
Take to a dry cleaner.

Ink - fountain pen
Washable items
As long as the ink is not permanent it should wash out relatively easily with a biological detergent.

Non-washable items
Sponge the area with a solution of white vinegar and water.

Ice Cream
Washable items
Sponge with warm water and then wash with a biological detergent. If after washing there are signs of a stain remaining, use a dry cleaning fluid.

Non-washable items
To remove the stain sponge lightly, then use a grease solvent.

Make-up - foundation / mascara
Washable items
Sponge with warm water and a little liquid detergent then wash as normal.

Non-washable items
Use a proprietary dry cleaning fluid.

Make-up - lipstick
Washable items
Sponge with methylated spirit and then wash as normal.

Non-washable items
Either take to a dry cleaner or use a grease solvent.

Metal Polish
Washable items
Blot up any residue using a paper towel, then sponge with white spirit and wash as normal.

Non-washable items
Blot up any residue using a paper towel, then rub the stain gently with white spirit.

Mildew
Washable items
Remove any residue that is loose by brushing, then rub with salt and a little water. When the salt has dried wash as normal.

Non-washable items
Take to a dry cleaner.

Milk
Washable items
Soak in cold water with a liquid detergent, then wash as normal. If after washing there is still a stain rub the area with methylated spirit.

Non-washable items
Sponge with warm water and liquid detergent. If a stain remains after drying use a proprietary stain remover.

Mud
Washable items
Mud should be left to dry completely before any attempt is made to remove the stain. When the mud is dry, brush off and wash as normal.

Non-washable items
When the mud is dry, brush off and remove any remaining stain with a dry cleaning solvent.

Nail Varnish
Washable items
Remove any stain with nail varnish remover (do not use on acetate). It is sensible to test the material before using nail varnish remover, then wash as normal.

Non-washable items
Take to a dry cleaner.

Paint
Most paint related stains occur as a result of decorating. To avoid stains, take care that you and surrounding surfaces are well protected from paint splashes and drips. Even if you are just going to 'touch up' a couple of window frames don't risk your best clothes: always change into something expendable.

Paint - emulsion
Washable items
Wipe off any deposit, soak in cold water and then wash as normal.

Non-washable items
Wipe off any deposit, then sponge with cold water.

Paint - gloss
Washable items
Wipe off any deposit, treat as quickly as possible with white spirit and then wash.

Non-washable items
Treat as above, but do not wash. If there is still a mark take to a dry cleaner.

Perfume
Washable items
Rinse in warm water and then wash as normal.

Non-washable items
If the item is particularly delicate take to a dry cleaner, if not treat with an equal mixture of water and glycerine, then sponge with warm water.

Perspiration
Washable items
Sponge with a weak solution of ammonia and then wash as normal.

Non-washable items
Sponge the area with a solution of white wine vinegar and water (5ml of vinegar to 250ml of water). If the stain persists take to a dry cleaner.

Scorch marks
Washable items
Light marks can be sponged with a solution of borax, then rinse and wash as normal.

Non-washable items
Light marks can be sponged with a solution of borax or glycerine.

Shoe Polish
Washable items
Remove any deposit, then sponge with white spirit or a proprietary grease solvent.

Non-washable items
Remove any deposit, then use an aerosol grease solvent. If any mark remains treat gently with white spirit.

Tar
Washable items
Sponge with eucalyptus oil from the back of the fabric or a special tar remover.

Non-washable items
Treat as above.

Tea
Washable items
Sponge off any residue, then soak in warm water with a biological detergent or borax solution and then wash as normal.

Non-washable items
Sponge gently with a borax solution, followed by clean water then blot dry. If the stain persists use an aerosol stain remover.

Urine
Washable items
Treat as quickly as possible. Rinse in cold water and then wash with a biological detergent. If it is an old stain it is not so easy to remove. To help, soak the item in a solution of water and hydrogen peroxide (ratio of 6:1) and then wash as above.

Non-washable items
Sponge with cold salted water followed by clean water.

Vomit
Washable items
Remove any deposit, then rinse in cold water followed by soaking in warm water with a biological powder. Wash as normal.

Non-washable items
Remove any deposit, then sponge with warm water with a few drops of ammonia added. Finish by sponging with clean water and blot dry. If the stain persists take to a dry cleaner.

Removing Household Odours

There are often never enough pleasant smells around like the aroma of freshly baked bread, honeysuckle and ground coffee. Air fresheners can combat many offending odours, but there will always be some that require special treatment.

Bathroom
Bathrooms frequently seem to contain unbreathable odours. Thankfully there is a quick remedy.

• Strike a match and let it burn for a while, then extinguish it. The unpleasant odour will soon vanish (provided the room doesn't explode).

Cigarette smoke
If you are not a smoker and someone has been smoking in your house trying to remove the odour will be a priority.

• A few drops of lavender oil is one of the best ways of removing the smell. If this fails try a bowl of water with three or four drops of ammonia in and leave overnight.

• Whilst people are smoking place a bowl of vinegar somewhere in the room to absorb some of the odour, or have a lighted candle in the room.

Cupboards
Cupboards should be tidied and the surfaces washed occasionally but if they do smell it is a good idea to empty the cupboard to find the cause. It is often due

to a food item that has worked its way to the back of the cupboard and gone mouldy.

● Clean with detergent and try placing a piece of activated charcoal in the cupboard.

Dustbins
The secret is to wash regularly and then rinse with disinfectant. Smells can to some extent be avoided by only putting rubbish that is in sealed bin bags inside the dustbin.

Fridge
Try to clean the fridge regularly and keep and eye out for food that should have been thrown out. If you are keeping very strong smelling food in a fridge always keep a lid on it.

● If your fridge has an unpleasant odour, first empty and wash with a solution of 1 teaspoon bicarbonate of soda mixed with 1 pint of warm water. Then place some baking soda in the bottom of the fridge, this should remove the offending smell.

Paint
A freshly painted room can produce quite powerful aromas. Certain paints require ventilation; when a bedroom has been painted it must not be used until all the fumes have gone.

● To help remove the fumes place a bowl of salt or an onion which has been cut in half in the room whilst painting.

Shoes

If you have a problem with smelly feet, the first thing to do is invest in a pair of charcoal impregnated insoles, they really work wonders.

● If you have a pair of shoes you wish to remove the smell from, try sprinkling the insides with baking soda (but remember to remove the soda before they are next worn).

Household pests

You always know when summer is on its way: the annual invasion of creepy crawlies leaves you in no doubt. This country has its fair share of pests, but at least we do not have some of the more exotic and terrifying bugs that are present in more distant parts of the world.

The average house and garden will be home to many thousands of bugs, animals and mites. As they say, prevention is better than cure, and it is true in this instance. Here are a few tips that should help to stop bugs and other animals making your home their home.

Many pests are attracted by the warmth of the house and food that is in it. They just love all those crumbs and sticky patches of jam that have not been cleaned up properly. There is not much that can be done about the warmth, but make sure that you keep your kitchen clean and tidy.

• Don't leave unwrapped food lying around, always keep lids on food, especially sweet things. There is nothing more annoying than coming down to breakfast to enjoy a slice of toast and your homemade marmalade only to find that a party of ants has beaten you to it.

• Clean your drains regularly with disinfectant, remembering it is harmful to pour hazardous products down a drain.

• Always keep a lid on your dustbin and clean it occasionally. The same applies to your kitchen bin.

Pest Repellents
There are numerous types on the market: sprays, powders, gels and aerosols. Choose one that is appropriate for the problem you are facing. Chemical agents should be used with care, especially if you have

young children and pets, so always read the instructions. Remember that some pests can be dealt with more simply . . . a rolled up newspaper is still perfect for fly swatting!

Common pests
There are many different types of pests found in this country. Many, such as earwigs, are not harmful, but most people prefer to have a pest free house.

Ants
These are a particular problem in summer and it is not unusual to see trails of them marching from the outside of your house to food sources on the inside: nothing seems to get in their way. If you can find their point of origin, which is hopefully the nest, you can try pouring boiling water into the hole. If this does not seem to work, purchase a specific product. Many of the products work by the poison being carried back to the nest by other ants thus causing genocide. Ant powder poured across their routes of entry into the house can effectively discourage them from crossing this 'barrier'.

Bees and wasps
These are also a problem in the summer months, but if they are not bothering you it is best to leave them alone. If you want to be rid of them buy a special spray.

One way of trapping wasps is to make a wasp trap, which should be put in the garden, near to where they are causing a nuisance. To make it: cut the top off a plastic squash bottle, and half fill the main part of the bottle with a sweet liquid. Put the cut off part of the bottle upside down on the main part. The wasps should then fly into the bottle through the funnel, but they should not be able to escape. If you find a wasps nest in your house or garden do not attempt to remove it yourself, contact your local authority for assistance.

Cockroaches
The horror story of any kitchen is the cockroach. They tend to be found in any unclean environment, and they can carry germs and viruses. To kill cockroaches buy a specifically prepared pesticide, but if they get to be a real problem contact your local authority, which will send someone out to fumigate the house.

Earwigs
Earwigs are actually harmless, but if they are in your house just sweep them up and throw them outside. If you want them killed, use an insecticide.

Fleas
Cats and dogs are the main carriers of fleas into the home. If you have fleas you will soon know about it: they leave an itchy bite! Check pets for fleas, and if you find any treat the animal with a flea powder or spray. Remember to treat the animal's bedding.

After spraying, fit the animal with a flea collar. If you still have a problem, there may be fleas in the carpets and furniture, so treat these and then hoover. After hoovering remove and destroy the hoover bag.

Flies

These are a common problem: they are annoying, unsightly and can carry many diseases. They are particularly prevalent in the kitchen, but a kitchen that is clean will have less of a fly problem. Make sure that no food is left lying around, just think what a fly has been treading in before it was standing in your food!

Remove flies with fly spray or use one of a number of natural remedies. Flies find certain smells unpleasant, including natural products such as lavender, rosemary and cloves which can be placed in the house to ward off flies.

Mice

Although many people keep mice as pets, they can also be an unwanted visitor. Although you might not actually see mice there are often signs. Look out for small black droppings and indications of chewing, as mice will gnaw through practically anything, including electric cables. You might also hear them scratching around. They might look cute but they can cause a great deal of damage as well as carrying salmonella.

• To rid yourself of the little rodents there are a number of choices. Buying a cat is one option, as they are naturals at catching mice. The only problem is that they have a habit of putting the dead mice on your bed in the morning as an offering. Not the nicest thing to wake up to!

• If you don't fancy this, buy a few mousetraps and place them in the areas where you think they 'hang out'. Humane mousetraps are available. These don't actually harm the mouse: they consist of little boxes with a trapdoor that falls shut once the mouse is inside, tempted by the food. You then simply carry the mouse to nearby woodland or wasteground and release it unharmed.

• If you have no luck with the traps then you will have to use a rodenticide. This a strong poison and should only be used as a last resort.

Moths
It is not the moths that do harm it is the moth larvae. They have a fluffy white appearance and have a habit of destroying woollen products such as jumpers and carpets, and other natural fibres. To remove the larvae try to brush off then treat with a special spray.

• Watch out for the larvae in the folds of material such as curtain linings or the hems of skirts.

• If the larvae is attacking clothes in a drawer try sprinkling some Epsom salts in the drawer, this should keep them away.

Rats
You don't want rats in your house. They carry disease and can give a nasty bite. Rats love filth, so a pile of rotting food is their idea of paradise. If you keep your house and garden clean you should never have a

problem. If you do receive unwelcome visits, it could be that your neighbours are not so tidy and the rats are enjoying life next door and popping over from time to time.

● If you have a rat problem, purchase some rat poison, but make sure that you follow the instructions carefully. Be extra cautious if you have pets or young children. If this does not work contact your local authority or pest control agency.

Spiders

Spiders are harmless and although they receive bad press and can turn hardened adults into quivering wrecks there really is nothing to fear. In fact spiders help to reduce the number of insects in the house, especially flies. The typical house is home to about two thousand spiders, although most will not be visible, choosing to live between floorboards, in the attic, between the walls, or behind furniture. If you wish to remove the visible spiders from your home, then don't bother killing them just pick them up with a piece of paper and throw them out the window.

Woodworm

If you are buying any second-hand furniture check for signs of woodworm: minute holes and small amounts of sawdust will be apparent. Woodworms are not fussy about which wood they attack, but if you bring an infested piece into your house you run the risk of it spreading to other furniture. If you suspect woodworm treat with a proprietary fluid.

Cars

If you ever have a puncture in the middle of nowhere and when you come to change the wheel you find the spare tyre is flat, you will come to appreciate the importance of regular checks on your car. If you fail to look after your car it is more likely that it will break down, leaving you inconvenienced. The other important reason for looking after a car is so that it is safe to drive.

Car Tips
● Have the car regularly serviced and check the levels of petrol/diesel, water and oil yourself on a regular basis.

● Check the condition of the tyres, including the spare, make sure they have adequate tread and are inflated to the correct pressure.

● Always carry in the car a torch, up-to-date road atlas, warning triangle, bottle of water, jump leads, first aid kit and a few essential tools.

● In the winter carry a de-icer blanket, bar of chocolate, candle, matches and a small shovel.

● Other useful items include spare change for the phone or parking meter, rubbish bag, umbrella, tissues, and a notebook and pen.

● Wash the car regularly, not forgetting to do the underneath.

Home Security

It is alarming how many burglaries occur every year: around three quarters of a million, and the figures estimated by the British Crime Survey put the figure at nearer one and three quarter million. These frightening statistics are the sobering reality for many. It is tragic that after working hard to buy your possessions someone can just come along and help themselves. Not only is the loss of property distressing, the intrusion into your home is for many a psychological experience that may take a long time to recover from. The best way to avoid being burgled is to take precautions, and although they will not guarantee your protection, they should improve your chances.

The majority of burglaries are committed by the opportunist thief, who will look for certain indicators in a house and then decide if it is worth taking a risk, eg. are there any windows left open, or is the house surrounded by tall fences or hedges giving plenty of cover? A burglar will look for the house that appears to be an easy target and has little opportunity of him being discovered.

Here are a few crime facts:

● About 50% of burglaries occur during the day.

● About 80% occur when there is no one at home.

● The rear of the house is the most popular point of access for burglars, either through the back door or windows.

Bear in mind that there are certain items that burglars tend to go for, and most of the time they are limited to what they can carry. Although there have been stories where thieves have left houses bare, including taking the radiators, sinks and toilets, fortunately thieves are not normally this organised. The following are among the most popular items stolen:

● Televisions
● Videos
● Cash / credit cards
● Jewellery
● Stereos
● Camcorders
● Cameras
● Computers
● Compact discs

There are two important areas that need to be looked at. The first is the security of your home. As the statistics show, the chances of being burgled are now too high merely to regard it as an unlikely eventuality. As Lord Baden Powell said to his scouts, 'Be prepared'. The more precautions you take the less risk you have of being burgled.

Here are a few security tips:

- Fit window locks to all easily accessible windows.

- A five lever mortice lock, plus a cylinder lock should be fixed to the front door.

- A lever mortice sashlock and a heavy duty bolt, should be fitted to the back door.

- Fit locks and secure bolts on all French windows.

- Keep tools and ladders secure so they cannot be used by burglars to help them gain access.

- Fit timer switches to lights. The more you have the greater the illusion.

- Do not leave valuable items in view.

- Remember to cancel milk whilst away.

- Inform neighbours if you are going away so they can keep an eye on your property.

- Join a neighbourhood watch scheme.

- Photograph valuables, so if you are burgled you have proof of what you owned.

• It is a good idea to keep the receipts of all valuable goods as it will help with the insurance claim. Keep them in a safe place, if they get stolen too it will make it harder to claim on your insurance and it will also benefit the burglar.

• Be extra vigilant at Christmas time as this is a favourite time for burglars to strike. There is nothing more distressing than having all your presents stolen, especially if you have young children who lose their toys.

If you are thinking about installing an alarm system, make sure that you get a reputable company to install it for you. There are many different services available, many charge an annual fee, and some of the more expensive alarms send a message to the police if the alarm is activated. Having an alarm is not a guarantee that you will not get burgled, but it may reduce the chances. Insurance companies usually offer a discount on homes that are secured to a certain specification. As well as protecting your home, thorough security could protect you and your family, and for many it provides a little peace of mind.

Allergies

There is almost an unlimited number of causes of allergies and over 10% of the population suffer from an allergy of some sort. An allergy is the body's reaction to a substance that it is sensitive to. Many allergies are caused by household matter such as dust, animals, various foodstuffs, soap and pollen. Household dust is one of the most common causes of an allergy. The symptoms vary from person to person, but include:

- Runny nose
- Rashes
- Sneezing
- Itching
- Swollen eyes
- Blisters

If you suffer from a dust allergy the less dust that you have in your house the less you should suffer. Dust and hoover all surfaces regularly.

If the cause of the allergy is a pet, then either the pet will have to find a new home, or you will have to try to keep the pet out of certain rooms, especially bedrooms, and off the furniture.

Food allergies are also common. Anything from peanuts to dairy products can cause allergic reactions in some people. The way to find out which foods are causing the problem is to 'cleanse' your system with a diet of rice for a few days. Plain rice does not normally cause any kind of reaction even in the most sensitive people. One at a time, bring back other foods into your diet, noting any symptoms as they occur. If done properly and under medical supervision, the causes of allergies should make themselves known as they are reintroduced to your diet. Take care when in the 'cleansing' stage to take supplements of all the necessary vitamins and minerals.

If you think that you might have an allergy, consult your doctor who will be able to arrange the best kind of test for a range of common allergies.

Barbecues

At the first sign of summer our barbecue is brought out of the garage and put to good use. There is something about cooking on a barbecue that makes even the humble sausage seem utterly delicious, appetites seem to double and they are a great deal of fun. One of the biggest drawbacks of barbecues in this country is the uncertainty of the weather: a barbecue ideally should be accompanied by sunshine and warmth, as they do not have the same appeal when it is raining.

Whether you are having a barbecue for four or twenty an element of organisation is required. Although there are various styles of barbecues available, personally I don't think you can beat the traditional charcoal burning type. You might be thinking 'is there any other type?' well yes, it is now possible to buy electric and gas powered models . . . these are certainly not for the purists.

Lighting the barbecue

Most barbecue enthusiasts have their own particular method for lighting the barbecue. Whichever method is used caution must be used as accidents can occur.

• Never use petrol or a similar fuel as it is extremely volatile and could lead to serious burns and its fumes can also taint the food.

There are two main types of charcoal: briquettes and lumps, and either can be used. To light the barbecue, use either special lighter blocks or fuel. Another alternative is to use kindling wood with a little paper. Once the barbecue is alight a footpump makes a wonderful set of bellows, just aim the nozzle at the glowing charcoal and pump gently. Once you have several pieces of charcoal glowing move unlit pieces on top of those that are hot. To get the barbecue up to cooking temperature normally takes about 30 to 40 minutes.

How much charcoal is used depends on the size of the barbecue and the amount you want to cook on it. If you are cooking three courses you will obviously need more charcoal than if you are cooking for one course. If it is a party make sure that you use enough - it is embarrassing only having enough heat to cook half the food, so it is always better to use too much. If you are cooking late into the night and it is getting chilly why not move the barbecue close to the table after you have finished cooking where it makes a wonderful heater?

● If when barbecuing you have too many flames, keep a bowl of water handy to douse the flames. Just flick some on the charcoal with your fingers. If you want to be really clever try using a plant spray.

● Although food always tastes wonderful when cooked on a barbecue (unless it's burnt to a crisp) there are extra ways to add to the flavour. Marinating meats such as chicken or pork can add extra flavour to your food or burn fresh rosemary on the barbecue.

Spring cleaning

There is cleaning and there is spring cleaning! The phrase *spring cleaning* is associated with cleaning on a grand scale, not your ordinary quick whizz with a Hoover and fleeting dust of a few surfaces. Every now and then a house requires a thorough overhaul. Everyday cleaning may keep your house looking superficially clean, but there are many areas that get neglected. How often do you clean under the beds or behind the cooker? Grime builds up in these places throughout the year, cupboards and drawers get full and messy, and the house generally needs sorting out.

Spring cleaning needs time and organisation, at least a whole day or longer if you have a large house. Attempting to clean whilst trying to look after young children is no easy task, in fact it makes it extremely difficult. If you have pets you will have to deal with an extra burden. It is advisable to see if you can arrange to do your spring cleaning when the children are not there, this will mean that you should be able to work a great deal quicker.

Here are some hints as to how to make your spring cleaning session run smoothly:

● Before commencing with the cleaning check that you have all the materials you will need, for if you have to nip out to the shops half way through your cleaning it will waste valuable time.

● Make a list of the order in which you are going to clean.

Carpets

Carpets are still the most popular floor covering in this country, but they do require looking after if they are to remain looking smart. Carpets can last for years if they are well looked after, but their longevity is normally decided by the quality of carpet. In general a thick carpet will last a lot longer than a thin one.

The main problem with carpets is that they suffer from being trampled on day after day. If you don't allow shoes to be worn in the house you will save a lot of wear and tear on the carpet. Wearing shoes in the house also brings in mud and grime which is ground into the carpet. To reduce the amount of mud brought into the house place door mats behind front and back doors.

If you decide that your carpet is looking grubby then you can shampoo it using a special carpet shampoo. The shampoo can either be applied with a brush or a household carpet shampooer. Before starting, test a hidden area of carpet to see if the colour runs, if it doesn't run continue.

An alternative method of cleaning carpets is to hire a specialised carpet cleaner or pay someone to come and do it for you. These carpet cleaning machines are very effective at removing long standing grime. If you are hiring a machine and cleaning the carpets yourself make sure that you read the instructions that go with the machine. As with shampooing do a test on a hidden area before starting, in case of colour runs.

The cleaner works by forcing hot water into the carpet which is then sucked out. One of the most important points to remember when using the machine is that damage can be caused to the carpets if they become too wet.

Bathrooms
Cleaning the bathroom is mentioned in detail elsewhere in the book.

Showers
Clean the showerhead on the outside and on the inside. They are susceptible to a build up of limescale deposits which impedes the flow of water. Use a descaler to remove the limescale. Check that the shower hose has not got any leaks.

Shower curtains
The main problem is these is that they can become mildewed, especially if the bathroom is damp. If the mildew is very bad it might be worth replacing the shower curtain.

● To remove mildew from a shower curtain wash with a mild solution of bleach and water. The problem of mildew can be avoided if the shower curtain is not pulled back after use, this means that the water can dry off, rather than becoming trapped.

Shower trays
• Clean with a cream cleaner and remove any bits of soap or hair that might be obstructing the waste outlet.

Sponges
A real sponge as opposed to the type used to wash a car needs looking after. After a while sponges can build up a slimy deposit, this slime can be removed by washing the sponge in a solution of vinegar and water.

Tiles
Most bathrooms have tiles as they protect the wall from water and moisture. But keeping them looking shiny can be a problem especially if the water is hard in your area as water marks can be left each time they get wet.

• Clean tiles with an ordinary cream cleaner or try using a solution of vinegar and warm water in equal parts. Remember the darker the tiles the more they will show up water marks and they will need more frequent cleaning.

Bedrooms
One of the main problems encountered with keeping a bedroom clean is how tidy it is kept. There are bedrooms where you will be lucky to catch a glimpse of the floor as it will be covered in clothes and shoes, while others are almost regimental in their tidiness, carefully folding and putting away clothing after it has been worn. There is no doubt that it is a hard

task trying to clean a room where the surfaces are not even visible!

Beds

A bed is one of the most essential pieces of household equipment, since we spend about a third of our lives in them. A good bed will normally give a good night's sleep, so it is worth investing in one that you find comfortable.

● It is all too easy to shove things under a bed when tidying up, so when it comes to cleaning under the bed you never know what you might find. There will normally be an assortment of odd socks, underwear, books, prurient magazines and a thick layer of dust. Clean the area beneath the bed and then try to find the corresponding socks to the ones you found there.

Duvets

These are a wonderful invention that make bed-making a much easier task. There are various types available. As well as coming in a variety of sizes they come in different weights and fillings. The warmth of a duvet is usually estimated from its tog rating. The average tog values range from about 10 to 15, with the higher value being the warmest.

The most expensive duvets are filled with down, next are the feather filled ones. The cheapest duvets are normally filled with synthetic fibres.

Always use a duvet cover as these can be washed easily but washing a duvet is not easy and should be avoided if possible.

If a duvet does need cleaning:
• Feather or down duvets should be taken to a dry cleaner. They must not be washed at home.

• A duvet that has a synthetic fibre can be washed if it is absolutely necessary. If you are washing it in a machine make sure that your machine can cope with the weight.

Pillows
A good tip to stop pillows from becoming stained is to use two pillow cases as it will give more protection.

As with duvets only wash pillows if necessary. The problem with washing pillows is that they take such a long time to dry.

Halls
The hallway of a house is usually subject to a great deal of abuse, as it is the junction that leads to all the other rooms. In the winter when there is mud about, the hall is the first place where muddy foot prints will be deposited. It is a good idea when considering a hall carpet to choose a dark colour which will not show marks as easily as a lighter one. A patterned carpet shows marks and stains the least, and those brightly coloured swirly patterns that were in vogue during the seventies are probably the best.

• If mud is brought into the house it should be left until it dries and then brushed off.

• Hoover the hall carpet, but if it still looks dirty then consider having it cleaned with a liquid.

• Take the doormat outside and beat with a stick. This usually produces clouds of dust so don't do it inside.

• Dust all the walls and lampshades. If the lampshades are washable take them down and wash them with a little washing up liquid. Let them dry before putting them back up.

• Clean light switches: grease marks can be removed using a cream cleaner on a damp cloth. Never use a wet cloth on any electrical fittings unless the power is off at the mains.

Paintwork
First of all dust the surfaces making sure that you pay special attention to the corners where dust and dirt can accumulate. Then wash the surfaces with washing-up liquid and wipe dry with a clean cloth.

Pictures
Remove pictures and dust gently. If the pictures are covered with glass, clean the glass with either a vinegar solution or a special glass cleaner. Having removed a pictures, clean the area that it has exposed.

Stairs
A loose stair carpet can be a hazard, so check that it is firmly attached. Then hoover thoroughly.

Kitchen

Appliances such as fridges, freezers, cookers, and washing machines need to pulled away from the wall. It is amazing what lurks behind these types of appliances. Apart from a thick layer of dust and dirt you might find long lost items of cutlery, egg timers, dinners, coins, or even a ring. Cleaning might be more rewarding than you think! Clean thoroughly behind and underneath the appliances.

Blinds and curtains

Venetian blinds are a dust trap and get greasy if they are used in the kitchen.

• If they are just dusty they can be wiped with a cloth and a little detergent, there is no need to take them down. However, if the blinds need more than dusting it is easier to take them down and clean them in the bath.

• If you have curtains take them down and wash them.

Flooring

Most kitchen floors have to put up with all sorts of spills, therefore it is important that the surface is suitable. If you have a carpet in your kitchen it will soon become messy, so it is advisable to replace it with a more practical material, such as vinyl flooring.

• Clean your kitchen floor on a regular basis before it becomes unsightly. If you have tiles on the floor clean the grouting as dirt can become trapped between the tiles.

Fridges

The fridge should be emptied and defrosted if necessary, then cleaned with a solution of 1 teaspoon of bicarbonate of soda in a pint of warm water.

● One important area that is often neglected is the rubber seals that surround the door. If you have ever worked in a restaurant you will know this is a favourite place for health inspectors to check as it is a notorious trap for dirt and mould. Clean all the seals on your fridge and freezer.

Extractor fans

An extractor fan can be very useful in a kitchen, especially if you are in the habit of cooking greasy fry-ups. They extract the air and expel it to the outside. The drawback is that they can become covered in grease and dust.

● Before cleaning make sure that you turn the power off to the fan. The fan will have an outer casing which should be removed first, and this can be cleaned in hot soapy water. The blades should be cleaned with a damp cloth. After cleaning make sure that you fit the cover back on tightly and that it is dry before it is switched on.

Cupboards

Clear out all the kitchen cupboards checking for any out of date items. Jars tend to get pushed to the back and can stay there for years. After removing all the contents clean all the surfaces with a cream cleaner, then rinse well.

Sinks

Stainless steel sinks should be cleaned with a stainless steel cleaner. Alternatively try using a damp, screwed up newspaper.

Holidays

To ensure that your holiday is all that you wish it to be, there should be an element of planning involved. Before booking the holiday there are a number of things to consider:

• Make sure that you can get the time off work.

• Choose a destination that will satisfy all the demands of you and your family. If you have children, check that there are adequate facilities to keep them amused, otherwise leave them behind!

• Before booking the holiday, shop around and compare prices: they do vary from company to company, even for two identical holidays.

• Check that you have adequate travel insurance.

• Check that your passport is still valid and that you have all the necessary visas.

• Make a photocopy of all travel details and keep it in a separate place when you travel.

• Don't forget to have all the correct vaccinations and remember to take anti-malaria tablets if they are required. If you are pregnant make sure that you seek advice from your doctor if you are planning to go to a far off destination. You might be advised to take extra precautions or not go at all.

• Before you leave for the holiday it is a good idea to read up on your chosen destination. There are many excellent travel guides available for almost every country in the world, offering an insight into the history, traditions, cuisine, weather and main attractions. It is always sensible to know a little about the country you are planning to visit, and it is only polite to be able at say at least 'please' and 'thank you' in their language. It is also important to be aware of the local customs, eg. what dress should be worn by women, whether photographs should be taken of the locals, how to deal with beggars etc.

• Arrange for any pets to be looked after either with friends or at a cattery or kennels.

• If you are driving abroad check that you are have the necessary insurance (a green card is the normal requirement, this extends your British policy to certain other countries).

• Have your car serviced in good time before you leave on a driving holiday. Breakdown cover can be extended to give protection in mainland Europe.

• Inform your neighbours that you are going away and ask them to keep an eye on your property. Leave with them details of where you are staying and a contact number.

• If you have lots of plants that need watering put them all in one place with instructions, so that whoever is looking after them will know their requirements and will not have to search the house hunting for hidden plants.

• Settle any bills that will need paying whilst you are away, because you don't want to come back and find that you have had the electricity cut off. If you have a key meter for your electricity, don't forget that if you don't have enough units to cover the time away your electricity will go off and if you have a freezer you will have a terrible mess to clear up on your return as well as having wasted money.

• Fill in an E111 form which can be obtained from the Department of Social Security. This entitles you to free health care in countries that are part of the European Union.

• Order foreign currency, travellers cheques as soon as possible. It can take some days to obtain certain currencies, so organise it a least a week before you leave. It is sensible to take most of your money in travellers cheques, only keeping a small amount of cash with you.

Holiday items that might need to be purchased:
Sun cream, sunblock, hats, sun-glasses, maps, phrase books, insect repellent, first aid kit, travel sickness tablets.

Cameras
Always take one more film than you think you will need, as it can be difficult obtaining film in certain countries and tends to be more expensive. If your camera uses batteries and you are not sure how old they are, replace them. I have been in a situation where I was in the Indonesia about to photograph an orang-utan when my camera failed due to a flat battery. This was a heartbreaking moment, as there was no chance of finding a battery of the type required and the camera was useless without one. This sort of experience teaches you to be organised the hard way.

• On leaving for your holiday don't get dressed up in your best outfit. It is essential to feel comfortable whilst travelling. If you are flying long distance don't have tight shoes on, as feet can swell during the flight.

Before you leave
• Water the plants in the garden, not forgetting hanging baskets. (summer only).

- Empty the fridge of any items that will not keep whilst you are away.

- If you are not a good traveller and feel sick whatever mode of transport you use, remember to take travel sickness pills before you leave.

- Remember to cancel your newspapers, milk, and other deliveries, and turn off the water.

- Secure the house, making sure that if you have any light timers they are in operation.

- If you have a burglar alarm and your neighbours will be entering your house whilst you are away, show them how to operate it before you go, and in case they don't fully understand write down the instructions.

Household Baby

If you are expecting your first child, after the initial shock of realising that you are going to become a mother there will normally be a period of panic. Pregnancy means being fat, being sick, getting tired, eating strange combinations of food and finally giving birth, so there is a lot to cope with!

When pregnant, advice will be given from a number of sources: friends, family, medical professionals, and even the girl in the chemist. Often the advice is conflicting which leads to even more confusion. There are other sources: health centres, books, and magazines so you will never be short of information. However, facts and figures are one thing, reality can be something completely different.

The planning involved with the expected arrival of a new baby is immense, but don't worry. It will get harder! There are all sorts of things to do, one of the most fun being the great name debate. Choosing a name is exceedingly difficult. Just remember to have some consideration for the child, if you name it after your favourite football team they are not likely to thank you in later life! *Emma is a nice name for a girl, by the way.*

The house must be prepared for the arrival of a baby and you must train your mind to the fact that you will have to take more care than normal. Babies and young children are naturally inquisitive and love to explore, therefore you will have to make the house as safe as possible. It should be said that although it is only natural to feel protective towards children, they are remarkably robust and you should not spend your time worrying excessively about their every move. As long as adequate precautions are taken they should come to no serious harm, though there will always be the inevitable tumble and bump on the head, but this is only normal.

● Children seem to love poking things, putting their hands through packaging in shops or worse still trying to put their fingers or your keys inside an electric socket. Fit socket covers to all sockets that they can reach.

● Fit locks on lowdown kitchen cupboards and the fridge.

● Keep medicine and harmful cleaning chemicals out of reach.

● If you have a real fire, use a fire safety guard.

● Fit stair guards to stop babies and toddlers from falling down the stairs.

Pets

Thousands of pets are mistreated in households every year. Having a pet is tremendous responsibility and with some animals having a life expectancy of well over ten years make sure that you are aware of what you are letting yourself in for before buying one. Whether your pet is a whippet, a budgie or a pot bellied pig, it will require love, care and expense, but will in the end be a worthwhile addition to any family.

If you are considering buying a pet think about the following questions.

● Are you prepared to look after the pet for its whole life? If the pet is for a child you could find that they get bored with it after a while and you have to take over the responsibility.

● Can you afford a pet? As well as cost of feeding, which is expensive if you have a larger animal, there are vet's bills, bedding, kennel or cattery fees etc.

● Having a pet can make life complicated. If you want to go away to stay with friends, you either have to get someone to look after the pet whilst you are away or you have to take it with you. This can put you in an awkward position.

● If you are thinking about buying a dog, are you prepared to walk it everyday, in all weathers?

● Is your house large enough to cope with a pet? If you have a two-up, two-down then buying a Great Dane would not be very practical.

Dogs

● It is not fair to leave a dog on its own all day long, so if there is no one at home during the day it is not advisable to have one.

● A puppy that is lonely can be comforted by placing a ticking clock wrapped in a towel in the puppy's basket. This simulates the ticking heartbeat of its mother.

● If you have children and are considering buying a dog, then it is imperative that you consider carefully which breed you buy. Breeds such as labradors are generally good natured and can put up with a certain amount of prodding and tail pulling by young children. Seek advice from a canine club or a vet about suitabilities of different breeds.

• After children have been playing with dogs it is advisable to get them into the habit of washing their hands.

• Puppies are born to chew: slippers, shoes, furniture, and magazines are common favourites. Try to remember to keep anything you cherish out of the reach of a young pup. One more serious point is that dogs can chew through power cables, so keep them hidden if possible. To discourage persistent chewers, buy a dog repellent spray and use it to spray onto furniture and electrical cables where the dog is likely to try to cut its teeth. The taste and the aroma should teach it to stay away.

• Dogs can be discouraged from misbehaving by teaching them to fear the sound and sight of a tin containing gravel. Whenever a dog does something wrong, shake the tin of gravel loudly close to the dog. The noise is unpleasant and should make the dog back away and stop whatever it was doing. They will soon come to associate this unpleasant sound with the sight of the tin, so leaving tins in strategic places can make them avoid those areas. If your dog is prone to jumping onto furniture while you are out of the house, for instance, a tin left on the smartest chairs will put a stop to such criminal activity.

Cats
• If you are considering buying a kitten, think about buying a pair as they like company and will be much happier.

• Before bringing a kitten home the house should be prepared. Kittens are particularly mischievous and to stop them escaping, make a habit of keeping doors and windows closed.

• A kitten should not be left alone for long periods.

• Cats have an annoying habit of scratching furniture with their sharp claws. To stop this occurring make a scratching post out of a piece of old carpet attached to a wall or chair leg. Try to train your cat to use it by placing its paws on the scratchpost and make scratching motions.

• It is not only children who like to play, so have a selection of toys for your cat's amusement. Make a mobile using cotton and a ball of rolled up newspaper and hang it in a place where they can reach it.

• A cat needs regular grooming, preferably on a daily basis. This will reduce the chance of it becoming a home to fleas.

Household Finances

Whoever is in charge of the household purse will know that although it is not quite on the same scale as running a small business, there is a fair amount of work involved in keeping the household finances in order. The idea is to make the income for the household balance the expenditure.

If you are haphazard with your finances and have little idea what is coming in and what is going out, living in the hope that you will have enough money to cover all the bills, then it is about time you became organised. A household which is organised with its finances will run a great deal more smoothly and should make your money go further than one which is not. If you are constantly going into debt because of poor financial management it will cost you even more money.

Budgeting
Household expenditure is divided into two main categories, *fixed costs* and *variable costs*.

The following are the most common fixed costs:
• Mortgage or rent
• Council tax
• Insurance
• Television licence
• Hire purchase instalments

With fixed costs the amount you have to pay and the date of payment are normally known in advance.

The variable costs are numerous, and their amount would normally change according to usage. These include:

- Food
- Electricity
- Gas
- Phone
- Car repairs and fuel
- Entertainment
- Travel expenses
- Holidays
- Sundries

The first step in the organisation of the household finances is to calculate the total income of the household. The next stage is to work out the total amount for the fixed costs. Deduct the second figure from the first to get the amount that you will have to spend on the variable costs. To help calculate variable cost expenditure use past bills to work out how much you spend, checking, for example, old electricity, telephone and gas bills.

If you write down a list of your expenses you should get a picture of how your income is spent. There will be certain unaccountable amounts but you should be able to account for most of it. The idea of keeping accounts is to control spending so that you don't end up in debt. By looking at the list of expenditure you might be surprised how much money you spend in certain areas: it is then time to think about ways of adjusting expenditure and hopefully saving some money.

Bills

Brown envelopes arriving on the doormat are normally junk mail or bills, both equally unpleasant. Your house will rely on many services from the utility companies such as water, electricity, and gas, plus the services of local providers like milkmen and newspaper deliveries. They will all need paying: if you don't you will find that their services are soon withdrawn, leaving you very much inconvenienced. In the case of the utility companies, if they disconnect their services because you have not paid your bill they will charge you when you eventually have the service reconnected.

However painful it is to look at the bills, it is essential that you do not hide them away in the vain hope that you won't have to pay them. Work out the order in which the bills need to be paid and arrange them on a clipboard where they will be a reminder to you. If you are having financial difficulties it is important you contact the people to whom you owe money. Generally people are more understanding if they are aware of the situation and will be more willing to extend the period of repayment.

Cars

A car is not only expensive to buy, maintain and to run, there is the added environmental cost which occurs as a result of burning fuel. There are a number of ways of cutting fuel consumption without actually changing your car:

• Don't warm the engine up while the car is stationary.
• Make sure the choke is pushed in as soon as the engine is warmed up.
• Empty heavy loads from the boot if they don't need to be there.
• Keep your tyres correctly inflated.
• Accelerate and brake gently.
• Use the highest possible gear available without making the car judder.
• Use motorway routes where possible. Continuous driving uses less fuel than stop/start urban driving.
• Keep to within the speed limits.

Borrowing money is expensive, so the less you owe the better off you will be. It is also sensible to have a emergency fund of money, as it is not possible to predict when your car is going to break down or get damaged. If you constantly spend up to your limit then in these circumstances you will find yourself in a tight spot.

Saving money

Good household management should include trying to make economies where possible without affecting the quality of life. There are hundreds of ways to save money, many of which not only save money but also save time and generally make life more comfortable.

Cutting the heating bill

The average size house will cost hundreds of pounds a year to keep warm and to provide hot water. Heating is very much a necessity due to the rather miserable climate of this country, but there are ways to make savings. If you consume less fuel not only will you be saving money, you will be helping the environment.

Top tips to save your fuel bill:
• By reducing the temperature of your thermostat by just one degree for the whole year, you can save on average up to 10% of your fuel bill for the year. You probably won't even notice the difference in temperature.

• Have your central heating boiler serviced on a regular basis. If it is not running efficiently it will be wasting your money and precious fuel. There is also the element of safety, as boilers can be dangerous if not maintained.

• If your boiler is old, say over 20 years, it will definitely be less efficient than the ones you can buy now. By fitting a new boiler you could save up to 30% on your fuel bill.

• Why not try to reset the timer so that heating comes on 15 minutes later and goes off 15 minutes earlier? You can try these things and if you find it uncomfortable you can always change it back.

• The more control you have over your central heating the more efficiently it should run. It is possible to purchase central heating programmers that give accurate control over the heating going on and off, and a variety of combinations with regards to whether water heating is required, or heating only, or both together.

Most houses only have one thermostat that estimates the temperature for the whole house. This is not a particularly efficient method as some rooms need to be warmer than others. For instance the living room will normally be required to be warmer than a bedroom. The solution to this problem is to fit thermostatic radiator valves, these monitor the temperature in each room a valve is fitted and adjust the heat according to the set temperature.

If you don't have central heating and you are using electric heaters, make sure you use Economy 7 which is cheap off-peak electricity. A special meter has to be fitted for Economy 7, and a small quarterly charge is made, but it will save a great deal of money.

Keep in the heat
To retain the heat in a house it needs to be sufficiently insulated, otherwise the warmth will soon disappear, resulting in more heat having to be produced. There are a number of key areas that are prone to losing the heat and these should be considered first.

● Loft insulation - Lofts should be insulated to a depth of 150mm. If you already have insulation but it was fitted several years ago, check the depth of it, as it might be too thin. Loft insulation can be bought from most DIY stores and can be fitted without too much trouble.

● Fit draught excluders around the edges of doors and windows, as up to 40% of heat is lost through these areas.

● Double glazing is a very effective method of keeping in the heat, cutting out draughts, and reducing external noise.

● If you don't have double glazing and can't afford it, then fit secondary glazing which is cheaper, and although not as effective as double glazing it still helps.

● One step down from this is to buy special cling film which can be fixed to the window frame and stretched tight by blowing it with a hairdryer. This is a very cheap form of secondary glazing, but is not as efficient as the other methods.

• Place tin foil behind radiators to reflect the heat away from the wall and out into the room.

• Lag pipes and both the hot and cold water tanks. The hot water tank is the most important as heat is lost quickly if it is not insulated.

• Have old fireplaces boarded up, and block gaps between floorboards and skirting boards.

Saving Electricity

• Remember to turn off light bulbs and other electrical appliances when not in use. Electrical appliances that are left on standby, such as televisions, are still using electricity.

• Fit energy-saving light bulbs instead of standard filament bulbs. An energy saving bulb will last eight times as long as a conventional bulb and will use less electricity.

• Don't over use appliances such as electric heaters, tumbledriers and dishwashers, as they all consume vast amounts of electricity.

Saving money on food

It is very easy to overspend on food purchases, but if you are on a budget you will have to learn how be strict with yourself. Here are a few tips on how to cut down your food bill.

• Buy loose fruit and vegetables as these are a great deal cheaper than prepackaged items.

• Buy the supermarket's own brands as they are cheaper than branded products.

• Buy what is on 'special offer' and build a menu around these items.

• Try to avoid buying ready prepared meals as they are much more expensive than preparing them yourself. They are, however, useful for occasions when you don't have the time to cook.

Washing hints

Washing Machines

The washing machine is one of the most essential of all household appliances. Washing by hand, although necessary for certain items, is a gruelling and time consuming task. To get the most from a washing machine it has to be used and maintained correctly.

Most washing machines that are now sold are automatic, as opposed to twin tubs. The advantage of automatic machines is that once the washing is in they can be left, while a twin tub requires a lot more effort and time.

● Read the instructions fully for a new machine. They are becoming more and more advanced, and yet they still have a habit of making socks disappear.

- Keep the hoses at the back at the machine free from any kinks, so the water can flow freely in and out of the machine.

- Do not use more than the recommended amount of washing powder as it will not get the clothes any cleaner.

- Clean the rubber seal of the door on a regular basis. Bits of fluff and hair often get trapped between the seals.

- If a dispensing tray is used for detergent and fabric conditioners it can get clogged up so remove it and clean thoroughly.

Washing tips

Machine washing
- Check all labels before washing to make sure that they are suitable to be washed and the recommended temperature.

- Sort laundry into groups, ie. coloureds, whites etc.

- Take extra care with new coloured items as they are more than likely to run. It is normally advisable to wash them separately for two or three washes. To test the colour fastness wash the item with an old white piece of material, if the material takes the colour then obviously the item is still running and still needs to be washed separately.

- Treat any stains before washing as once they have been in the machine they may be harder to remove.

- Rinse any heavily soiled items before washing.

- Check pockets for coins, pens, tissues etc.

- Any items that have tears in should be mended as washing can make the tears worse.

- Never overload a washing machine, especially if they are heavy items such as bath towels.

Special cases

Certain materials require special care, such as wool and silks. Read the care labels before washing. They usually need hand washing with a specific hand washing detergent.

Wool

Woollen items have to be hand washed unless they say on the label that they are machine washable. Some washing machines have a special programme for woollens.

- The main problem with washing woollens is that they are prone to losing their shape. If the garment has buttons or a zip, such as on a cardigan, do it up, as it will help to keep the garment in shape.

- After washing a woollen garment it should not be wrung, but gently squeezed.

- To dry, lie on a towel on a flat surface. They can be hung up to dry if they are light enough.

- Garments must be kept out of direct sunlight when drying as it could cause them to fade.

• If a woollen item has shrunk it can sometimes be stretched back to the original shape with a little gentle persuasion.

Silk
Silk is a luxurious but delicate fabric that needs special care.

• Handwash with a suitable detergent in warm water, be gentle with the material as it is prone to tearing when it is wet.

• To dry, gently squeeze out the excess water and then place between two towels and pat dry.

• It is always easier to iron when still damp.

• If you have a heavily soiled silk garment it is advisable to take to a dry cleaner.

Ironing tips
• Always check the care label of items before starting and select the correct temperature for the material.

• Iron clothes in batches that require the same temperature setting, this will save time by not having to adjust the temperature every few minutes.

• Always use distilled water in a steam iron. Ordinary tap water will cause scale to build up in the iron.

• Check that both the iron and the ironing board are clean before use. If the iron is dirty it can ruin clothes.

• Cover the ironing board with an aluminium cover. This helps to reflect the heat and generally makes ironing easier.

• When ironing an item do it in a logical pattern, going from one section to another.

• It is easier to iron clothes when they are slightly damp. Bear this in mind when tumbledrying: if clothes are left in for too long they can be difficult to iron as they are so dry.

• Using a fabric softener makes clothes easier to iron.

• Iron in a position that you find comfortable. Sitting down in front of the television is a favourite place.

• Never wear clothes that have been freshly ironed as they will crease as soon as you put them on, wait till they have cooled.

• Hang items of clothing such as shirts and dresses after ironing, don't place on them the backs of chairs or sofas.

• If you are uncertain of the material you are about to iron, always use a low setting just in case.

• On fabrics such as jeans that are severely creased try using a fine spray of water. A small indoor plant sprayer is ideal for this purpose.

Garden hints

Compost
No serious gardener should be without a compost heap, and each gardener has his or her own ingredients which they feel gives the perfect result. For those of you who are unsure what exactly compost is - compost is basically a fertiliser produced from garden and household waste, this does not mean old washing machines and plastic bottles. A compost can be produced from a wide variety of sources, the following being the most popular:

- Grass clippings
- Vegetable scraps
- Egg shells
- Old leaves
- Plant cuttings.

To make an effective compost requires patience as the compost is formed as a result of bacterial action. It is possible to purchase special agents that speed up the rotting process, but it will still take several months before the compost is sufficiently rotted to use.

Indoor Gardening
Plants and flowers can give a wonderful feeling to a house, and no home should be without a few plants and vase of flowers. The main drawback of having plants is that they require looking after, if they are not cherished they will soon die. There are so many choices of plants for the home that it would be

impossible to give suggestions as to what should be bought, and it is recommended that a specific indoor plant book is purchased.

If your fingers are not even remotely green and you have trouble keeping a plastic plant looking healthy here are a few botanical tips.

• Buy plants that look healthy, avoid plants that appear to be wilting.

• Check for signs of pestilence before buying.

• Check before buying a plant that it will be suitable for your house. Some plants may require constant warmth, so if you have no heating think again.

Having bought a plant always read the instructions as to what environment it prefers, how often it should be watered and fed etc. Too many people fail to realise that plants have many different requirements, which must be fulfilled if the plant is to flourish. It is no good neglecting a plant and then flooding it with water, a plant needs regular care.

• Never place plants close to a radiator or on top of a television. Plants prefer an even temperature.

• Keep the leaves free of dust and spray leaves occasionally with water, except cacti.

• If a plant is growing unevenly it may be because one part is getting more light, to avoid this turn the plant round occasionally.

• Don't leave plants on a window sill with the curtains drawn, especially in winter, as the gap between the window and the curtain gets very cold and is damaging for plants.

Flowers

If you are lucky enough to have freshly cut flowers in your home it is essential that you do everything that is possible to prolong their life.

• Flowers should spend as little time as possible out of water.

• If you are cutting your own flowers try to cut them in the evening, as they will last longer.

• Prepare flowers before placing in vase. Roses should be stripped of thorns and a small split made in the bottom of the stem. This technique can be used on any woody stems.

•Most people have their own theory as to what is the best way of keeping flowers looking fresh: water is a good start, but added ingredients such as sugar, wine, charcoal, and aspirin are said to help.

• Keep the water fresh by changing it every couple of days, making sure there is enough water to reach all the stems.

Metric conversion charts

Many people find that their brain still functions in imperial rather than metric measurements, the following might help if you need to work out any conversions.

Conversion Formulae	Multiply by
Inches to Centimetres	2.54
Centimetres to Inches	0.3937
Feet to Metres	0.3048
Metres to Feet	3.2808
Yards to Metres	0.9144
Metres to Yards	1.094
Miles to Kilometres	1.6093
Kilometres to Miles	0.6124
Gallons to Litres	4.546
Litres to Gallons	0.22
Ounces to Grams	28.35
Grams to Ounces	0.03527
Pounds to Grams	453.952
Grams to Pounds	0.00220462
Pounds to Kilograms	0.4536
Kilograms to Pounds	2.205

Temperatures
To convert Celsius to Fahrenheit
Multiply by 9, divide by 5, then add 32.

To convert Fahrenheit to Celsius
Subtract 32, multiply by 5, divide by 9

Tyre pressures

lb/sq in	kg/cm2
10	0.7
12	0.8
15	1.1
18	1.3
20	1.4
21	1.5
23	1.6
24	1.7
26	1.8
27	1.9
28	2.0
30	2.1
33	2.3
36	2.5
40	2.8

Fuel

litres	gallons
5	1.1
10	2.2
15	3.3
20	4.4
25	5.5
30	6.6
35	7.7
40	8.8
45	9.9
50	11.0

Weights

Imperial	Metric
1oz	25g
2oz	50g
3oz	75g
4oz	100g
6oz	150g
8oz	225g
12oz	340g
14oz	400g
16oz	450g

Liquids

0.25 pint	0.5 pint	1 pint	2 pints
150 ml	300 ml	600 ml	1200 ml

Oven temperatures

Centigrade	Fahrenheit	Gas mark
100	200	Low
110 - very cool	225	1/4
120	250	1/5
140	275	1
150 - cool	300	2
160	325	3
180 - moderate	350	4
190	375	5
200 - mod hot	400	6
220	425	7
230 - hot	450	8
240	475	9
260 - very hot	500	10

Index

Other books from Summersdale

VOLUNTARY WORK
ABROAD

Corinna Thomas

Foreword by
Mark Tully
BBC India Correspondent

New edition

£5.99 (paperback)

The Busker's Guide To Europe

How to make a fortune from your talents (and get a free holiday!)

Stewart Ferris
£5.95 (paperback)

DON'T
LEAN OUT OF
THE WINDOW!
Surviving Europe on a Train

The Inter Rail travelogue

"It's nothing but bad language, bad taste, absent morals, and a damning indictment of modern youth. I loved it!"

Stewart Ferris & Paul Bassett
£4.95 (paperback)

How To Chat-up Women

AS SEEN ON TV
Matt Mountebank
£6.99 (paperback)

Classic Love Poems

£10.99 (hardback)

How To Become A Millionaire

Advice and business plans for the serious entrepreneur

CHARLES RYDER

£6.99 (paperback)

REAL
SELF DEFENCE

GEOFF THOMPSON
£12.99 (paperback)

How To Save Money

RICHARD BENSON
£5.99 (paperback)

THE STUDENT GRUB GUIDE

Over 150 easy and popular recipes for students

New edition
ALASTAIR WILLIAMS
£4.99 (paperback)

These books are available through all good bookshops. In case of difficulty, write to us enclosing a cheque or postal order payable to SUMMERSDALE PUBLISHERS. Please add £1 p&p per book if ordering from within UK, £3 p&p per book if ordering from overseas.
Send to: Summersdale Publishers, PO Box 49, Chichester, PO19 2FJ, England